Frank Crowley

THE FIGHT FOR
MALAYA

THE FIGHT FOR
MALAYA

The Jungle War of Maurice Cotterill

R.W. Holder

Editions Didier Millet

First published in 2007 by
Editions Didier Millet Sdn Bhd
25 Jalan Pudu Lama
50200 Kuala Lumpur
Malaysia

www.edmbooks.com

Printed in Singapore

ISBN 978-981-4217-20-0

Note on currency: Dollar amounts referred to in the text are
Straits Dollars, unless otherwise indicated.

Contents

Map of the Malay Peninsula in the 1940s

Gulf
of
Thailand

0   50   100 km

PERLIS

THAILAND

KEDAH

Kota Bharu

PENANG • Butterworth

KELANTAN

• Taiping

TRENGGANU

• Kuala Kangsar

PERAK • Ipoh

Batu Gajah •   • Cameron Highlands
        • Ulu Ringlet

South

China

Sea

Tapah •   • Kuala Lipis
    • Bidor
        • Jerantut

• Selim

• Kuantan

PAHANG

• Tanjung Malim

SELANGOR • Kuala Kubu

• Kuala Lumpur

Klang/Prt Swettenham

Morib Beach •

NEGRI
SEMBILAN

• Segamat

• Mersing

Strait of Malacca

MALACCA

N

JOHORE

SINGAPORE

Foreword

As I write this foreword, my thoughts go to the celebrations in Malaysia marking the 50th anniversary of Merdeka, 21 August 2007. It was on the same date back in 1957 that the era of colonialism ended in Malaya, and Sabah and Sarawak joined the Malay States to form the new Federation of Malaysia.

The road to independence was a long and winding one, and the two decades which preceded the big day were tumultuous. A whole generation of Malaysians were deeply affected by World War II and the Emergency which followed; and it gives me particular pleasure to be introducing a book which examines part of this story with new insights.

When Bob Holder told me that Maurice Cotterill's nephew had passed him his uncle's wartime diary, I became as excited as he was. Having played some part in the publication of Bob's earlier book, *Eleven Months in Malaya*—a personal memoir recalling the British Military Administration during the post-war period in Malaya—I knew immediately that we had to do something about Maurice's diary.

I can think of no more vivid way to encounter the realities of World War II and its aftermath than to read this book, which is not only based on a first-hand account written by someone who 'stayed behind' for the duration of the Japanese occupation, but sets the whole period in the context of decolonialisation, that momentous process that gave birth to some of the most dynamic nations in the world today.

I hope you enjoy reading *The Fight for Malaya: the Jungle War of Maurice Cotterill*, a remarkable portrait of modesty and courage, set against a formative period in the history of Malaysia.

ZARIR J. CAMA
Kuala Lumpur

Prologue

The camp where Maurice Cotterill and the Chinese band of robbers were living lay about a mile from the jungle edge, near enough to obtain food from the kampong but sufficiently remote for them not to be taken by surprise when an attack came. Although the gang did not maintain a standing guard on the only track leading to the camp, it was booby-trapped and an explosion gave them time to grab their guns and ambush any intruders.

The villagers knew where they were hiding and in the past had been able to send them warnings about any impending police action. Now the Japanese were seeking to control the countryside as they did the towns. They paid informers well and had started massacring villagers who supplied food to the guerrillas and bandits living in the jungle. Maurice knew that the next attack might be more serious. If the gang broke up, his Chinese companions could merge once more into the community outside. He, a European, could never leave the jungle.

When the Japanese army assault came, the gang received no warning. The men who carried their rifles were away on a raid. The attacking party was about 100 strong, with the Malay policemen leading the way so that they would trigger the booby traps and take the casualties rather than the Japanese soldiers. To resist them, Maurice and the Chinese had between them two pistols and two sub-machine guns. With the assault confined to a single path and impenetrable jungle on either side, they should not need more firepower.

After the first explosion, the Japanese soldiers halted and started firing into the trees at random. The gang had plenty of time to vacate the camp and move to their ambush positions. After they had killed nine of the intruders, the Japanese withdrew. Knowing that they would soon be back in greater strength, the gang abandoned the camp and moved to another which they had prepared further into the jungle. They had shelter there from the rain but getting food would be more difficult.

Two days later a larger detachment of Japanese attacked them in the new camp. This time they were surrounded and had to slip away singly, taking only their weapons with them. They now had nowhere to shelter from the tropical rain and they had lost their only source of food. It was August 1943. Maurice had been a fugitive for 20 months since the Japanese invasion. He would not see another European for 14 months or leave the jungle for two years.

1

Rubber Planting and Prewar Society

John Maurice Cotterill, always known as Maurice, was born on 11 November 1905 in the village of Ashley, near Market Drayton, in the English rural county of Shropshire. He was one of seven children, two of whom died young. His father was headmaster of the village school, a solid Victorian building which is now in use as a health clinic, and the family lived in a large detached house which still stands at the other end of the village. As befitted his profession and religious conviction, the teacher brought up his children to be honest and industrious. It was a teetotal household. Under paternal influence, Maurice and his brother went so far as to sign the pledge not to touch alcohol, which was one undertaking that, in an otherwise honourable life, Maurice did not keep.

After attending the grammar schools in Market Drayton and Brewood, Maurice went to Reading to study agriculture in what was then a College attached to London University. As a talented cricketer and tennis player, he spent more time playing games than attending lectures. Sending a son to college was a heavy financial burden for a village schoolmaster with a large family, especially for one who had just retired. As his final examinations grew near, Maurice viewed a confrontation with the examiners with growing trepidation. In those days those who had neglected their studies would not just be awarded a lower grade but could actually fail the examination. That was not an outcome which was likely to receive parental approval back in Ashley.

At that juncture, in 1926, Maurice saw a vacancy advertised for an assistant manager on a rubber plantation in Malacca. He had shown, through his choice of course at Reading, that, unlike three of his siblings, he did not want to become a schoolteacher. The starting salary at that time for a European assistant manager in Malaya was around £450 a year, or considerably more than a newly qualified professional man could expect to earn in Britain, and twice what a locally recruited employee would be paid for the same job, if he had been given the chance of applying for it. There was also the excitement and novelty of going to live in a far-off and exotic country. Against that had to be balanced the four-year absence from home, separated from family by a long sea voyage, and a lack of female companionship during the first tour at least. Young planters were forbidden to marry before their second tour and discouraged from entering into extramarital sexual arrangements with local women of whatever race. When the Japanese invaded Malaya in December 1941, Maurice was still a bachelor.

British candidates seeking an appointment in the Malayan Civil Service (MCS) usually had academic qualifications, preferably from Oxford or Cambridge, and were selected after sitting a competitive examination held in London. A result of this method of recruitment, which was also a barrier to entry for local applicants, was that by 1941 only 27 Malays had been promoted to membership of the MCS after serving in the locally recruited, and less well paid, Malay Administrative Service. The British MCS officers were, however, of a generally high standard and usually proved competent District Officers. Few colonial civil servants who achieved senior rank stayed in the same country and someone promoted to Governor may have known little about the country he was sent to govern and been unable to speak the local language.

Unlike the government service, British-owned firms were happy to take on young Britons lacking academic achievement, provided they showed other attributes. Class distinctions, or snobbery, among expatriate staff, or their mems, still existed despite the oceans separating Malaya from the British Isles. Family background and articulation of speech were considered important. A Scotsman with his classless brogue was more acceptable than an Englishman speaking with a regional accent. Personal recommendation helped, because the new arrival had to live in an isolated community and be able to get on well with the other Europeans. Sporting ability was taken as an indicator of suitability for colonial life and this must have been a factor, along with his unfinished agricultural studies at Reading, which favoured Maurice.

More jobs than usual were available for expatriates in Malaya and elsewhere in the British Empire in the early 1920s because of World War I. Between 1914 and 1918 young Britons from Asia and Africa had left their colonial jobs to enlist, travelling back to Europe or serving in local regiments which were then posted overseas. Although the authorities in Kuala Lumpur had asked Europeans not to volunteer for service in France, some 700 British expatriates had done so, and around 200 did not return. The war had also led to a five-year gap in recruitment. It was still generally accepted, in British-owned firms, that there were managerial skills so complex that only a European could perform them, despite the manifest evidence, in Singapore and Malaya as elsewhere, that commercial ability was not a British monopoly.

Maurice started as Assistant Manager on the rubber estate in Malacca and by 1941 he had become Acting Manager of the Kuala Reman rubber estate in Pahang. He went back to Britain on leave in 1930, in 1934, and again in 1939, returning to Malaya on 11 November some weeks after war with Germany had started. While away, he regularly sent gifts back to his family and Philippa Cotterill, his only daughter, still possesses some letters sent to him by his mother, albeit somewhat ragged after spending nearly four years in his pocket in the jungle.

Taking a long leave in Britain involved up to eight weeks at sea and paying a substantial fare. In addition, the financial depression which lasted from 1929 to 1932 affected the rubber market as it had every other business and industry. The imposition of quotas on the production of latex can be interpreted either as a fiendish plot by greedy financiers in London or as an attempt to save all producers in the peninsula, British, Malay, and Chinese, from going out of business, in the same way that the oil-producing nations today seek to create a stable market. Managers also had their salaries reduced and, rather than return to Britain, some expatriates preferred to take their long leave in Australia. Maurice's immediate superior in Pahang, Vincent Baker, the manager of the Sungei Lembing tin mine near Kuantan, had earlier married an Australian whom he met there. Others, such as Vincent's assistant Brian Tyson, sent their families on leave to Australia, and that is where Tyson's wife and two young children were when he went into the jungle with Maurice in December 1941.

A plantation manager's day, and that of his assistants, started before sunrise. Working through junior supervisors, each tapper was allocated 400 trees from which to gather latex during the morning. Other manual tasks included the repair and maintenance of roads and bridges, which were often damaged by heavy rainfall; supervision of the tree nursery; clearing jungle for new planting; and weeding between the trees, especially to keep tough grasses at bay. Most estates had a sick bay or hospital and a shop. They also had their own workshop or 'factory' for the treatment of the latex with acid so that it could be more easily transported. When the latex was delivered to the factory, each tapper's contribution was weighed to prevent illegal trading and for the calculation of wages. All of these activities—the repairs, the nursery, the replanting, the hospital, the shop, the factory, and the office, were the responsibility of the manager, quite apart from running the business and reporting to his superiors. He also acted as arbitrator to settle disputes among the staff and as policeman to punish petty crime.

Chinese or Indian clerks usually ran the office and the store. As a race, the Chinese, who tended to be excellent gardeners and growers, found the tedium of rubber-tapping uncongenial. The tappers were normally Tamils or Telagus, both male and female, who preferred the security of employment in Malaya, however repetitive, to the poverty of life in southern India. On some estates children as young as eight years old worked beside their parents. The day which started early ended early, except for the clerical and household staff. The manager's domestic servants, other than the cook, were usually Malays. They included a *syce* or chauffeur, a cook, a *mali* or gardener, a house 'boy' or two for general duties, a sanitary man, and an *amah* or *ayah* for the children. On special occasions, other assistance would be provided by using people living in the tappers' quarters.

The European manager and his assistants lived in comfortable bungalows on the estate. The other employees had less commodious accommodation. Many of the tappers were single men and lived in one room. There was seldom adequate provision for the children's education, leading to a literacy rate of under 30 per cent among the population as a whole in 1941. Partly because of the isolation of individual estates but also because of regulations restricting union activity, the wage rates and conditions of employment were in effect dictated by the employers. Although the Malayan Communist Party (MCP), which was dominated by Chinese, had been founded in 1930, its leaders were imprisoned in 1931 and other adherents sent back to China, leaving no national organisation in a position to negotiate effectively on behalf of the tappers. In effect, an estate resembled a semi-feudal society in which the manager was the Lord of the Manor. Many managers were benevolent and well-meaning and others less so.

The local club was the haven to which a planter and his family resorted at the weekend. Away from Singapore and Kuala Lumpur, membership was open to all those of European descent and to others who managed to secure election. Apart from the eating and drinking, there might be facilities for team sports such as cricket, and individual games like tennis. Transient celebrities, such as the author Somerset Maugham, were lavishly entertained when they visited Malaya and elected to tell the world of a luxurious and decadent lifestyle in a way which was unfair to their hosts and misleading to their readers. To portray planters and their wives as nothing more than irresponsible hedonists made a better story than describing the reality of expatriate life—the long working day, the enervating climate, the isolation, the responsibility, and the expertise the job needed, even among those who had not passed the examinations set by the Incorporated Society of Planters. To that could be added, for the young planter, the lack of female companionship, and for those with children of school age, the years when their families were apart, even if the children were able to attend boarding school in Penang or the Cameron Highlands rather than be sent to be educated at 'home'.

The Kuala Reman Rubber Estate, where Maurice lived and worked in 1941, was near Kuantan in the state of Pahang. Kuala Reman Rubber Estates Ltd was owned by the same parent company as the Pahang Consolidated Company Ltd, which operated the only tin mine in Malaya. The mine was a massive enterprise, producing 27,000 tons of tin between 1924 and 1941. It had some 6,000 employees, of whom 27 were European expatriates, working under Vincent Baker's management as the Big Master, or *tuan besar*. As he had been considerate to his employees during peacetime, they were to show respect for him by refusing to betray him during the war. Baker had gone to Malaya in 1911 after graduating from the Camborne School of Mines in Cornwall. In 1930, at the height of the depression, instead of laying off staff or, as happened elsewhere, sending men back to China, he retained the surplus labour in civil engineering projects and in reclaiming land from the jungle for horticulture.

Vincent's Australian wife had suffered from ill health while living in Pahang. After the First World War she had gone to Britain with Vincent and the children to meet his family. The visit had not been a success. Vincent's father, the Rector of Dunstable, had followed the biblical precept to multiply, although, unlike his son, he had not gone forth. Two of his other sons had been killed in the war but the Rectory still housed a large and clannish family which appeared to exclude this Antipodean intruder. She and Vincent decided to separate and she took the three children with her when she returned to live in Australia.

When he returned on leave alone to Britain in 1935, now senior manager at the mine, Vincent invited his much younger sister, Nona, a music teacher, to return with him to Kuantan to act as his companion and hostess. Nona Baker and Maurice were to be, with Dugald Stewart of the Argylls, a planter called Chrystal, and an official in Kelantan called Creer, the only Britons who took refuge in the jungle in 1941 to survive there until August 1945. A very few others, such as Frederick Spencer Chapman, the author of *The Jungle is Neutral*, were evacuated to India before the occupation ended. The majority were betrayed, were captured by the Japanese, or perished of disease or starvation. The exception, the anthropologist Pat Noone, was murdered by a member of the *orang asli*, the tribesmen living in the jungle, who coveted Noone's Sakai wife. As we will see, Nona ended the war as a full member of the Malayan People's Anti-Japanese Army (MPAJA).

Pahang was in the 1930s ill-served with roads and the European community in Kuantan was tiny, with most of the men being unmarried. Nona loved the long sandy beaches and the life as her brother's hostess, with occasional trips to Singapore or, more often, to Ipoh, on mine business. Her entertainment was sometimes on a lavish scale, especially when the Sultan of Pahang came to dine, arriving with his own cook and food taster, and 40 other attendants. Returning with Vincent from leave in Britain in 1937, she was aware of the growing tension in Malaya caused by German aggression in Europe and Japanese adventures in China and Manchuria. Even in the mine, labour relations were less harmonious than they had been, although a visiting communist organiser lost his audience as soon as Vincent marched on to the scene. She, Maurice, and all the other expatriates in that remote region knew that the happy security and privileged life they had enjoyed was coming under threat. All were confident that the British could defend Malaya against a puny enemy such as the Japanese and that the fortress of Singapore, on which the enormous sum of £60 million had been spent over two decades, was impregnable. But they knew that there was likely to be fighting before that victory was won.

Spencer Chapman is another European, along with Nona, Vincent, and Brian Tyson, who features in Maurice's story. He was a mountaineer and explorer and had arrived in Singapore in September 1940, a month after the authorities had decided to set up a school for the training of parties of soldiers to remain behind enemy lines for sabotage and the provision of intelligence in the event of an invasion. The No. 101 Special Training School had students for operations behind enemy lines in Thailand, French Indochina, Hong Kong, and Burma, as well as in Malaya. Chapman was appointed Second-in-Command and was still in Singapore on 8 December 1941, when the Japanese invasion force landed at Kota Bharu and the first bombs fell on the city.

Ten days later the school opened its door to members of the Malayan Communist Party, its leaders going from prison direct to the classroom. These politically-motivated Chinese were to become its most enthusiastic and effective pupils, and were to form the nucleus of the MPAJA. A subsequent course, with Nationalist Chinese students, had not finished before the Japanese landed on Singapore island. Its students were to fight valiantly against them under a policeman called John Dalley in a unit named Dalforce.

Before we look at those exciting events, and Maurice Cotterill's participation in them, it may be helpful to see how the British had acquired a dominant role in the government of the peninsula, in return for which they had undertaken its security and defence from aggression.

2

Britain and Malaya

The adage goes that trade follows the flag, but, with the British Empire, the reverse was usually the case. The East India Company, based in London since 1599, leased Penang as a trading post in 1786 at a rental of $6,000 Spanish per annum. In 1819 one of its employees, Stamford Raffles, who had been a progressive governor of Java when it was taken by the British from the Dutch during the Napoleonic Wars, used the rivalry between the Sultan of Johore and his relatives (who ruled the Riau islands) to negotiate a treaty granting the Company another trading post on the almost uninhabited island of Singapore. A third Malay enclave, which the Company acquired in 1824, was Malacca, which had been colonised by the Portuguese in 1511 and had passed into Dutch rule in 1641.

So long as the East India Company enjoyed a monopoly over trade between India and China, involving mainly opium in one direction and tea in the other, the trading posts were profitable. Malacca had been a flourishing settlement when ceded by the Dutch and both Penang and Singapore developed into substantial colonies. The three territories in the Straits were initially controlled as part of the Bengal Presidency. With their remoteness and growing importance, in 1826 the Company gave them administrative independence, forming a fourth Presidency, so that Penang ranked alongside Bombay, Madras, and Calcutta as a capital city. When, however, the monopoly over the China trade ended in 1833, the new Presidency found it hard to raise enough revenue to meet its costs. Faced with something of a white elephant, the Company reverted to its former arrangement, placing what was known as the Straits Settlements again under the control of Calcutta.

To the north of Malaya, in a treaty of 1826 Britain acknowledged Siamese suzerainty over Kedah, Perlis, Kelantan, and Trengganu. These four States were subject to somewhat tangential Bangkok rule. Between them and the three Company settlements lay a number of Sultanates in which the rulers were seldom strong enough to control piracy and lawlessness, their right to the throne being often in dispute. Only in Johore did the ruler, despite disputed succession, have sufficient authority to maintain a relatively stable government, in part because of its proximity to Singapore.

In 1858, following the Indian mutiny or war, all the territories administered by the East India Company passed to the control of the India Office in London. Because they were geographically distant from the sub-continent, Penang, Malacca, and Singapore were in 1867 designated Crown Colonies under the direction of the Colonial Office in London. In Whitehall and Westminster, politicians and civil servants initially tended to view the acquisition as an encumbrance rather than a benefit and officials serving in the colonies were repeatedly discouraged from harbouring any ideas of territorial aggrandisement in the peninsula. This was a policy with which they did not always agree and an injunction which the local officials sometimes ignored.

The opening of the Suez Canal in 1869 gave the Straits Settlements a strategic importance. The shortest route from Europe to China and Japan now ran through the Straits of

Malacca and round Singapore island. Military considerations apart, the fact that the settlements were no longer in a geographical backwater greatly improved opportunities for trade. Trade cannot prosper unless life and property are protected. By the early 1870s the tranquility of Penang, with its large Indian population, was being threatened by disorder amounting almost to anarchy developing in the potentially rich state of Perak on its southern border. This was a situation in which the Governor of Singapore felt he had to intervene.

Sultan Ali of Perak had died in 1871, leaving a disputed succession. In the fighting which followed, thousands of refugees from the state took refuge in Penang and Province Wellesley, its territory on the mainland. Two Chinese factions had cornered the profitable tin mining. They also controlled the supply of indentured labourers and profitable provision of their leisure activities which involved opium and gambling. Apart from the unrest among the Malays, the Chinese were engaged in an equally violent dispute involving mineral rights and other issues. In January 1874, their leaders, threatened with military intervention from Penang, agreed to submit their differences to a British official for arbitration. Under the resulting deal, the two sides dismantled their fortifications and agreed that all arguments about mining rights should be settled by a British Resident.

The agreement between the Chinese and the British had to be ratified by the Sultan, but there was, for the moment, no Sultan. To resolve that difficulty, the Governor from Singapore summoned the Malay chiefs to a conference on the island of Pangkor, with a British gunboat and soldiers in attendance to help concentrate their minds. On 20 January 1874 the parties signed what became known as the Pangkor Engagement, a document which was to establish the future direction of British involvement in Malaya for the next 80 years. The fact that the English and Malay versions were capable of differing interpretations did not alter the basic premise.

The Engagement provided that the Sultan of Perak should accept a British Resident whose advice should be asked and acted upon on all questions other than those touching Malay religion or culture. Although the Resident had no executive power, he would in effect rule through the Sultan, and this model was subsequently followed in those States which accepted British Residents, other than Johore. One of the three British Commissioners appointed to arbitrate on the commercial disputes in Perak was a young official called Frank Swettenham, whose long career in the peninsula and life-long respect for the Malay people, tinged with condescension, were to contribute to the development of the new nation.

None of the subscribers to the Engagement was particularly happy about it, apart perhaps from Swettenham and his local colleagues. The Colonial Office accepted it reluctantly as a *fait accompli*, despite the fact that it contravened British government policy. The newly appointed Sultan owed his elevation to his willingness to sign the Engagement, but in obtaining a throne he lost his independence, and that of his successors. The squabbling Chinese were no longer their own lawmakers and enforcers in an anarchic society and would have to eventually stop treating their indentured immigrant workers, whom they controlled through debt bonding, as slave labour, although it would not be until 1893 that the last shackles were removed and the infamous Discharge Ticket System was made illegal. This was how potentially the richest state in the peninsula passed, for better or for worse, into British control.

Tin was mined in Selangor also, and in the nine small states which were to unite as Negri Sembilan. As in Perak, the succession to the throne in Selangor was in dispute. The state was lawless and one of the industries was piracy along the coast and up the rivers. In July 1873 a trader with interests in Selangor tin had informed the British that there was a possibility that the rulers might ask for protection from a European state, preferably Britain but failing that Germany. The response from London followed the usual line: 'Her Majesty's Government have, it need hardly be said, no wish to interfere in the internal affairs of the Malay States. But ...' there was a duty to rescue them from anarchy and restore order. ('But' is a very useful word for diplomats in these circumstances.) This duty Singapore undertook with the assistance of three gunboats and in August 1874, the Sultan, who had been following events in Perak, formally asked for the appointment of a Resident. The British used similar diplomacy in Negri Sembilan, with the same ultimate effect.

Thus with Johore still independent but bound to them by treaty, the British established *de facto* control over the western side of the peninsula from Penang to Singapore. On the eastern side of the mountain range which divides the country lay Pahang, the only independent state between Johore in the south and the Siamese territories in the north. Here also the British, along with other foreigners, had commercial interests and, even if they did not want to annex the state themselves, they wished to deny that opportunity to anyone else.

Pahang also was rich in minerals and during those years suffering from the apparently endemic succession difficulties of a Malay state. In addition to the usual crowd of European adventurers, the Maharaja of Johore had acquired some concessions there and enjoyed certain influence over the Sultan due to royal inter-marriage. Until 1885 the Maharaja was unhelpful to the British in their attempts to gather Pahang into their imperial fold. He then concluded a fresh treaty with them whereby he became a Sultan and agreed not to intermeddle in the affairs of his neighbours. Despite the loss of support from Johore Bahru, the Sultan of Pahang continued to stand out against having a British Resident until August 1888 when the Sultan of Johore persuaded him that he had to give way.

Swettenham had been involved, as we saw, in Perak immediately after the Pangkor Engagement. He was appointed Assistant Resident in Selangor in 1874 and thereafter remained closely associated with the States on the western side of the peninsula which had accepted British Residents. Part of Pahang's reluctance to conclude a deal with the British was because Swettenham's arrogance as a negotiator in 1886 had offended the Sultan. There were also those prepared to fight against a loss of independence and resented paying taxes annually. Until he became the first Resident-General of the Federated Malay States, Swettenham had no authority in Pahang.

There were sound administrative and fiscal reasons why the 'Protected' states which had accepted a British Resident should cease to be controlled independently from Singapore and be governed in effect as a federal country. Swettenham, as the first Resident-General, became responsible direct to London rather than to the Governor in Singapore, although this chain of command was not something he was quite so happy about when he himself became Governor in 1901. The manner in which their Rulers were harried or persuaded into giving their consent to the Federation in 1896 followed the pattern seen previously when constitutional changes were proposed by the British. For the Rulers, the Federation was another tooth in the ratchet whereby they lost authority to the British. They especially resented the ending of their right to final jurisdiction in legal matters, a constitutional change which contravened the provisions of the Pangkor Engagement.

Long-running discussions between Bangkok and Singapore, which led to Siam surrendering its dominion over the states of Perlis, Kedah, Kelantan, and Trengganu in 1909, completed the acquisition of territory in the peninsula under British control and established the boundaries of the modern nation. Suffice it to say that, squeezed between the predatory French in Indochina and the persistent British in Malaya, the Siamese played a weak hand with great skill over many years and a gunboat sent to Kota Bharu as part of the posturing was Siamese and not British. Thus, with Johore bound by treaty not to interfere in the affairs of its neighbours or to go to war without British permission, the political map of the peninsula had been fixed. The mélange of Crown Colonies, Federated States, unfederated States, and Johore survived until the arrival of the Japanese. The economic consequences of the British presence were no less significant.

In a climate of anti-colonialism, which pervades British

thinking today no less than that of those living in its former colonies, the benefits brought by a benign imperialist are easy to forget. Most British achievements, inventions, and discoveries were not confined to the Empire but shared with the world at large. The works of William Shakespeare, Isaac Newton, William Harvey, Adam Smith, John Locke, Charles Darwin, and their like are common property. Medically, all are able to benefit from inoculation against smallpox, from knowing how cholera and malaria are transmitted, from the aspirin and, in modern times, from penicillin. Inventions such as the flush lavatory, hydraulics, the steam engine, the locomotive, the railway, textile machinery, the blast furnace, the electric motor, the slide rule, tarmacadam, the cine film, the refrigerator, the computer, the jet engine, radar, and others of similar importance are accepted without thinking about, or giving credit to, the inhabitants of the far-off islands where they originated. It might have perhaps been better for mankind if others, such as splitting the atom, the tank, and television had not been thought of, but the world is a better place through being able to communicate in the English language.

One important British innovation at least owed its inspiration to Singapore, when the Samuel family, who exported shells to Europe, used the hull of a ship to convey paraffin on the return voyage rather than carrying it in 40 gallon drums, thereby introducing the tanker and the logo of a petrol company to the world. There were other British discoveries which brought particular benefits to the peninsula.

European planters, many moving from Ceylon, had grown coffee and sugar cane in Malaya, as well as indigenous crops, prior to 1900. In 1896 the bee-hawk moth ravaged the coffee plantations. A decade earlier, in 1887, a Scottish veterinary surgeon called John-Boyd Dunlop had fitted the wheels of a child's tricycle with inflatable rubber tyres. His invention coincided with the international development of the internal combustion engine. Thus the arrival of the motor age stimulated a huge increase in the demand for rubber. Another Victorian Briton, Henry Wickham, had smuggled 70,000 seeds of the tree *Havea brasiliensis* from Brazil to the botanical gardens at Kew near London. Kew sent the saplings of the rubber trees to Singapore where the celebrated botanist Henry Ridley devised an efficient way of collecting the latex. From 1900 onwards rubber became a staple crop in Malaya. By 1930 British-owned and managed estates grew 756,000 hectares of rubber and small-holders grew 540,000 hectares.

As we saw, the Chinese had been active in Malayan tin-mining before the British assumed political control. Smelting required more capital for equipment than primitive mining methods and after 1896 that activity was taken over by the British. (They carelessly left for the Japanese a newly commissioned smelter at Butterworth when they fled in 1941.) Between the wars the British commenced mining with bucket dredgers, each machine replacing the labour of 2,000 workers. Here again the increased capital cost was greater than most Chinese employers were able to fund and control of much of the industry passed to the British.

Rubber trees take seven years to mature which means that those developing an estate need a deep purse. Another British innovation of the 19th-century was the joint-stock company, enabling small investors to subscribe to the capital of a large enterprise with limited liability. Between 1903 and 1912 the London Stock Market saw the flotation of 260 such companies associated with Malaya. Frank Swettenham, in retirement, was often appointed Chairman. Within Malaya itself three British banks, with the Hong Kong and Shanghai Bank prominent among them, were able to provide traders with the facility of short-term credit through bills drawn on London, thus enabling them to handle international trade more easily. British merchant houses based in Singapore, such as The Borneo Company, Guthries, and Jardine, Matheson, acted as merchants, shippers, and agents facilitating the global distribution of Malayan produce.

Economic development needs good communications. It was here that Swettenham proved himself an effective operator. In 1872 it took him three days to travel from Klang to Kuala Lumpur by boat, a journey so uncomfortable that he and his companion decided to walk back through the swamps. The return journey took them 12 hours, and they were lucky not to have been captured and have their heads stuck on poles, as happened to other Europeans who chose to use the same path soon after. Construction of a railway between the two towns started in 1883 and the line was opened for full service on 1 January 1887, two years later than the completion of the line between Taiping and Port Weld. By the end of the century railways provided the communication system needed for the growing economy, although the Sultan was unhelpful about the line through Johore, and the causeway between the peninsula and Singapore island was not constructed until 1924. Without the

Federation the stretches of track laid piecemeal in different States before being joined up might not have chosen the same gauge. Nor would all the individual states have been able to finance the development from which they jointly benefited.

The infrastructure could not have been built so quickly and comprehensively without healthy public finances. In 1882 the revenue from land tax in Selangor amounted to a paltry $1,810. With Swettenham as Resident, the establishment of law and order, and improved communications, planters moved in. In 1883 the revenue had risen to $25,738 and by the end of the decade the surpluses in Perak and Selangor had risen to the extent that the government was not just able to finance roads and railways: other services costing huge capital sums were undertaken, such as irrigation to stimulate the growth of rice by mainly Malay farmers.

In the days before the imposition of penal inheritance taxes, a social custom aiding British global development and prosperity was primogeniture. The eldest son kept the estate or farm, while his brothers had to make their way in the church, the professions, commerce, or the forces. Islamic land inheritance law tended to lead to the creation in Malaya of uneconomic units as the land was shared among siblings. The establishment of large estates could not take place satisfactorily without a change in the laws governing tenure. The British were clumsy and unsuccessful in their early attempts to introduce reform and it was not until 1897 that a Federal Land Enactment was introduced, granting long leases on estates of over 100 acres. Malay Reservations continued to provide secure tenure of land for farmers until the Japanese occupation.

Under British tutelage, and to Britain's financial benefit, shanty towns like Kuala Lumpur and Ipoh became cities, swamps were drained, dry lands were irrigated, roads and railways were built, piracy and lawlessness were suppressed, estates were planted, forestry was managed, hospitals were built, and public health was safeguarded. Generally speaking, Malays dominated farming and the production of rice, the Chinese prospered in tin mining and commerce, the Tamils worked on rubber estates, and other Indians were traders. There were no bars to foreigners owning and operating substantial businesses, including plantations and extractive industry. The Japanese, for example, were involved in mining millions of tons of iron ore, along with manganese, bauxite, and wolfram, all essential for the construction of the fleet which controlled the seas in 1941.

The British were the administrators, managers, and servicemen, and their most important obligation was to defend the country against aggression. In this they failed, thwarted by the ambitions of another island race.

3

Japanese Imperialism

The long road which led to the Japanese invasion of Malaya can be traced back into the 19th century, or even two centuries earlier when the Shoguns decided that, to preserve the structure of Japanese society, there should be no contact with aliens. There were sporadic occasions when men from foreign ships went ashore. This only caused alarm if they drew attention to their presence, as happened when a British crew started a fight after visiting the brothels of Nagasaki in 1808, leading to the disgrace and suicide of the Mayor. It was left to the American Commodore Perry in 1853 and 1854 to show to the Shoguns, who ruled the country under the Emperor, that the coming of steam meant the end of isolation.

Nineteenth century political chaos in China facilitated the development of a Japanese empire beyond the home islands. Chinese concessions to westerners, and the resulting damage to the structure of its society, served to reinforce Tokyo's determination to keep foreigners away from Japanese shores. The island of Formosa, now Taiwan, was taken from China in 1895 and Korea, which had been under Japanese control since 1896, was formally annexed in 1910. In the meantime, in 1904, the Imperial Navy, based on the British model, had comprehensively defeated the Russian fleet. The Russians had sailed half way round the world for the fight, mistakenly engaging British fishing boats in the North Sea on the way.

Participation in World War I on the side of the Allies brought Japan its reward in the granting of a Mandate over former German colonies in the Pacific. With the Marianas, which lay strategically between Hawaii and the Philippines, the Marshall Islands and the Carolines all in Japanese hands, this largess following the Treaty of Versailles was something America had cause to regret in 1941.

After 1918, Britain and the United States viewed with alarm the growing Japanese naval power. The Washington Naval Treaty in 1922 imposed on Japan a tonnage restriction in capital ships amounting to only three-fifths of that reserved for the American and British fleets. The western logic behind this ratio was that Britain, and to a lesser extent the United States, had to station naval units in geographically separate theatres, while the Japanese fleet could be concentrated in one. For its part, Tokyo regarded the denial of equality with London and Washington as a national insult, and thereafter evaded the provisions of the Treaty by falsification of the tonnage of new launchings, by the incorrect classification of warships, and by whatever other subterfuge might come to hand.

In 1921 the Crown Prince, Hirohito, became Regent, succeeding as Emperor in 1926. It would seem that few in the West accepted that in the 20th century a technically advanced nation of over 50 million people could believe in the concept of a god/king who combined this dual role with that of chief priest of the national religion. The reality was that, as monarch enjoying absolute power, Hirohito could take advice from the ministers he appointed and be warned of any potential risks; however when he chose to move to a sacred chamber and speak in a high-pitched voice in archaic language, called the Voice of the Crane, he became a god, whose commands had to be obeyed without question. This was the voice which the vast majority of his subjects were to hear for the first time in August 1945.

The most effective check on the absolute power of the Emperor was the privilege invested in the ancient court family of Fujiwara of pointing out that a policy he was inclined to adopt might not be in Japan's best interest. Prince Fumimaro Konoye, who had since 1921 been the head of the Fujiwara family, was not opposed to Japanese conquest in China because he saw it as preferable to conflict with Japan's other traditional enemy, Russia. Nor did he oppose further military aggression to the south. But he warned against Japan becoming involved in a long war with western powers, and especially in one against the United States.

Continuing to benefit from the chaotic political situation in China, in 1931 Japan occupied much of Manchuria. In 1932, ignoring the toothless protestations of the League of Nations, from which Japan withdrew in 1933, Hirohito sent his troops into the rest of Manchuria, and moved into Inner Mongolia in 1937. In 1936 his army had become involved in an all-out but inconclusive fight with Soviet Russian forces on the Mongolian border. When the conflict with Russia was renewed in 1939, the Red Army under Marshall G.K. Zhukov inflicted such heavy losses on the Japanese in the battle of Khalkin-Gol that the Emperor decided that further hostilities against that enemy were best avoided.

There had been among Hirohito's advisers two schools of thought, one advocating expansion of the Japanese empire to the north, and the other wishing to conquer the countries to the south, and especially the Philippines, Malaya, and the Dutch

East Indies. By 1939 the United States had agreed to grant
independence to the Philippines, which had been ceded to it by
the Spanish after the war of 1898. The archipelago remained
under American protection and its nascent army was
commanded by the American General Douglas MacArthur. The
political situation in Malaya, as we have seen, was complex but
economically Malaya was a British possession and the British, in
return, had assumed an obligation to protect it against any
aggression. The Dutch East Indies were ruled as a colony from
the Netherlands. In these territories, and especially in what is
now Malaysia and Indonesia, could be found the minerals, oil,
rubber, and rice which Japan needed militarily, industrially, and
to feed its growing population. Invasion of the Philippines would
involve war against the United States. Attacking Malaya or the
East Indies would mean conflict with Britain or Holland without
necessarily involving America.

By 1937 Hirohito had decided that future Japanese
expansion should be to the south. The first necessity was to assert
greater control over China and to end the concessions granted
to the westerners in Shanghai and other Treaty Ports. Japan
had in 1930 lost control over its former protégé,
Chiang Kai-shek, and the Emperor resolved to destroy
Chiang's Chinese army by moving out of Shanghai to capture
capital Nanking. On 15 August 1937, using the Voice of
the Crane, Hirohito appointed General Matsui Iwane
commander of the expeditionary force, with instructions that his
troops should act with such ferocity that the Chinese people
would be cowed, the Chinese army would be scattered, and
Chiang Kai-shek would be persuaded to return to his former

allegiance. This policy involved not just ruthlessness towards those who fought in uniform, none of whom were to be taken prisoner. The army was to devastate the city of Nanking and terrorise its civilian population as a warning to others who might consider opposing the Japanese.

Some senior staff officers in Tokyo viewed these tactics with misgiving, fearing not for innocent Chinese civilians but rather that the discipline of Japanese soldiers might suffer if they were ordered to rape, loot, and burn at will. Matsui was a sick man, as Hirohito knew, and to ensure that his orders were carried out the Emperor appointed a member of the imperial family, his 'uncle' Lieutenant-General Prince Asaka, to oversee what was to become known as the Rape of Nanking, an orgy in which 80,000 soldiers ran wild for three days after the city fell on 12 December 1937, and then continued less intensely until 19 March 1938 when the last female victim was raped by a Japanese soldier within an American missionary compound.

Westerners living in Nanking, including Chiang Kai-shek's German military adviser General von Falkenhausen, told the world about the Japanese rampage. The ruthlessness fell not solely on the hapless Chinese. The day before the city fell, Japanese artillery on the banks of the Yangtze shelled a British gunboat, the *Lady Bird*, which was ferrying British refugees from Nanking to safety, killing a British sailor. The following day Japanese aircraft attacked and sank the clearly marked American gunboat, *Panay*, which was also carrying refugees from the city, killing two of the crew and severely wounding 14 other Americans. Britain and the United States issued protests and received apologies, not from the Emperor or Prime Minister but from Vice Navy Minister Yamamoto Isoroku. Significantly, the officer responsible for the attacks, Colonel Hashimoto, was not reprimanded and in 1939 became director of the Imperial Rule Assistance Association, the Japanese equivalent of the Nazi party in Germany. Yamamoto was to lead the attack on Pearl Harbor in December 1941.

Despite the military disaster and horror of Nanking, Chiang Kai-shek, after moving his government to a new capital city, carried on the fight. The mood of the Chinese people hardened against the invaders, thereby involving Tokyo in a war which could never be won. The Japanese army did however suffer heavy casualties in Nanking. The incidence of venereal disease was so severe that the troops were in future supplied with 'comfort girls', or prostitutes, at the ratio of one to every 40 soldiers, to avoid such casualties.

By occupying the Netherlands and driving British forces out of continental Europe, German aggression and military success in Europe had strengthened the Japanese position in the Pacific. Only the countries within the British Commonwealth and Empire (with the exception of Eire, which still owed allegiance to King George VI) continued to oppose Germany, albeit with moral and material support from the United States. On 9 September 1940 the German emissary Stahmer met the Japanese Foreign Minister Matsuoka in Tokyo to agree the terms of a treaty between Germany, Italy, and Japan. They were obliged to communicate in the only language which they had in common, which was English, and it was also in English that the Tripartite Pact was drawn up, and then discussed and agreed in the presence of the Emperor on 19 September. The Pact was signed by Adolf Hitler in Berlin on 27 September. Under its terms, Germany and Italy retained a free hand in Europe while Japan had the same freedom in the Far East. The only reservation among the Japanese negotiators came from the navy where the Chief of Staff, Prince Fushimi, warned that at all costs war against the United States should be avoided.

The fall of France had meant the isolation of its colony in Indochina, where the Governor-General had declared its allegiance to Vichy rather than joining the Free French. He was not informed of an agreement which had been made on 20 August 1940 between Matsuoka and the Vichy ambassador in Tokyo granting the Japanese military facilities in Indochina, including use of the naval base at Camranh Bay. On leaving the imperial conference on 19 September and with the Emperor's approval, that very evening Matsuoka telegraphed an ultimatum to Hanoi saying that Japan would invade unless the agreement made with Vichy was implemented within three days. Isolated, and having no support or guidance from Petain's government in France, the Governor-General capitulated. So it was, that even before the formal signature of the Tripartite Pact, Tokyo had secured the access and the bases from which to stage the occupation of Thailand in preparation for the assault on Malaya and Burma.

The Tripartite Pact expanded with the accession of Yugoslavia, Bulgaria and other states under German threat or occupation in the Balkans. This is not the place to discuss the Italian invasion of Greece on 28 October 1940. The significance of this far-off campaign to events in Malaya lies in the decision in March 1941 by the British General Wavell to send three

British Divisions to support the Greek army. This obliged Hitler to divert to Greece troops destined for Barbarossa, the invasion of Russia. In a campaign lasting three weeks, the two German corps destroyed the Greek army and drove out the British. But those three weeks were critical. The starting date for Barbarossa was delayed for the same period until 22 June 1941, with the result that the Wehrmacht arrived at the gates of Leningrad and Moscow three weeks later than might have been, by which time the Russian winter brought them to a halt. Thus Japan's traditional enemy, Russia, survived, to extract its revenge in August 1945, to facilitate the victory of the communists over Chiang Kai-shek in China, and so indirectly to provide support for the Malayan Communist Party.

On 25 July 1941 the Japanese Major-General Sumita arrived in Saigon to set up a military headquarters and Tokyo sent a further 8,000 troops to Phnom Penh in Cambodia. Washington responded by condemning the aggression and started moves to freeze all foreign Japanese assets. Early in August, President Roosevelt and Prime Minister Churchill met at sea off the coast of New England and in the following three days hammered out what was to be known as the Atlantic Charter, which expressed their joint aim of disarming all aggressors, allowing self-determination to all colonial people, and placing the United States firmly, if not actively, at the side of the British Empire in its fight against the Axis powers and, by implication, against Japan. At the same time the Australian government announced that it would not tolerate any further military aggression by Japan in the Pacific region.

Prime Minister Konoye knew that war against the British

was inevitable, but persevered in seeking a solution which would maintain the neutrality of the United States. Negotiations with Washington, through diplomatic channels and through the American Bishop Walsh, who had gone to Tokyo in an attempt to stop the expropriation of mission properties, intensified in October. The sticking point came with Washington's insistence that the Japanese should cease their aggression in China. The assault on Malaya, long agreed as a matter of policy, had been finally ordered by Hirohito on 6 September, to commence on 15 October. On 14 October Konoye asked Walsh to return at once to America to tell the President that, without concessions from Washington, he would resign and Japan would go to war against the United States.

Konoye's last-minute diplomacy exasperated both the Emperor and his War Minister, Tojo Hideka. On 17 October Hirohito dismissed Konoye as Prime Minister and appointed in his place Tojo, who remained Minister of War and Home Minister. Tojo postponed the attack on Malaya for a month, in part to see if Washington would back down now that Konoye had been dismissed. Having broken the Japanese diplomatic code and so able to read Tokyo's instructions to its Ambassador in Washington, Roosevelt knew that further negotiation was pointless and that war with Japan was inevitable. It was no longer a question of whether but of when.

The preparations for the assault on Malaya had been ongoing since the decision to attack to the south had been made in principle five years earlier. Japanese nationals in Malaya and Singapore had been recruited and trained as spies. Where necessary, skilled operatives were introduced as, for example, at the critical Kota Bharu air base where the station barber was a Japanese army Major in radio communication with the invading forces. The maps issued to the Japanese troops included tracks and other features in far greater detail than those available to the defenders. When Dato' Haji Mohamed Yusof Bangs, otherwise known as Bill Bangs, a member of the Kelantan Volunteers, ventured across the border into Thailand just before the invasion, he discovered that four previously derelict airstrips had been cleared and petrol dumps had been established to refuel incoming aircraft. On Tokyo's instructions, in November 1941 the remaining 4,000 Japanese citizens resident in Malaya left for home, apart from those charged with espionage.

From late July 1940 the General Staff had given General Yamashita the right to select the best veterans from fighting units elsewhere and give them two months of intensive training for the campaign in Malaya. Others were chosen for service in the East Indies and the Philippines. The navy rehearsed sea-borne landings from craft which had been developed in operations on the Chinese coast. Building a facility on the island of Phuket in only three weeks, the airforce ensured that it could continue to dominate the battlefield without capturing British airfields. No detail was overlooked. At sea, on land, and in the air, the Japanese forces were trained and ready.

The Japanese had long recognised that avoiding a foreign presence in Japan did not mean that they should also reject western technology. Under Hirohito, industrial development received a further impetus. Once war had started, it was to be as big a shock to the British that their vaunted *Spitfires*, and their *Spitfire* pilots, were no match for the Japanese *Zero* fighters, as it was to the Americans that Japanese naval equipment and training was superior to their own, especially when it came to the bombing of ships and the reliability of torpedoes. As the defenders of Malaya were soon to discover, the same thoroughness had been applied to equipping the army, and training it in the art of war. Practice makes perfect and the Japanese soldier, sailor, and airman had been practising for five years or more.

Having once admired the British, Hirohito now saw the country as a loser, driven out of Europe, including Greece and Crete, and with its Russian ally facing imminent defeat. From accepting an insulting apology from a lowly official for the attack on the *Lady Bird* in 1937 to cravenly agreeing to shut the Burma Road on 15 July 1940, thereby cutting off sea-borne supplies to Chiang Kai-shek, the British had shown their weakness and need to appease the aggressor. The day of reckoning had arrived. As for the Dutch and the French, they had already been taken care of by his German ally and their colonies were there for the taking.

In 1901 Prince Konoye Atsumaro had chosen the name East Asia All-One-Culture for the anti-western nationalist society and university he had founded in Shanghai. His philosophy had influenced such diverse luminaries as Sun Yat-sen and Chiang Kai-shek in China, Mahatma Ghandi in India, and U Nu in Burma. As a logical development, Tokyo promulgated the establishment of a Co-Prosperity Sphere which would include all countries in Southeast Asia which had been under western colonial oppression, protected by an outer ring of island fortresses. Faced, however, with the practicalities of conducting military operations against the Anglo-Saxon powers, Tojo refused to take seriously the concept of equality between the liberated peoples and their Japanese liberators. As each territory was conquered, the Japanese retained political control, imposed military rule, and managed its economy.

Before the war there would have been some popular support for the suggestion that Malaya, Indochina, Vietnam, and Indonesia should not have been controlled by European colonial powers, however benevolent, and that their resources should not be enjoyed by foreigners. If these countries were individually too weak to obtain their freedom, was it not logical that Japan, the military and economic giant of East Asia, should afford them assistance? The Emperor, himself a noted marine biologist honoured in Britain as a Fellow of the Royal Society, ruled a nation where universal education had resulted in a literacy rate of 99 per cent. Might not an Asiatic master be preferable to Europeans?

Only in Burma, whence 30 senior nationalists had visited Tokyo early in 1941 asking for help in obtaining freedom from British rule, did the liberating armies, or conquerors, not alienate the native population. When Tojo presided over a Greater East Asia Conference on 5 November 1943, claiming that 'the nations of Greater East Asia are bound by indissoluble ties of blood', too much of that innocent blood had been shed for his audience to accept his stated desire 'to secure stability in the Greater East Asia area and to create a new order on the basis of wealth and happiness for all'. In 1944 Hirohito, facing defeat and seeking help from any quarter, established a Greater East Asia Ministry not under Tojo's control.

But, as we shall see, by then it was too late.

4

Refuge in the Jungle

Maurice Cotterill was, like most European planters, a member of the Federated Malay States Volunteer Force, a part-time military unit to which all races belonged. On 1 December 1941, with the invasion imminent, he was told that, as Acting Manager, he should remain on the Kuala Reman Estate when other Volunteers were called away for military service. These men, with their local knowledge and language skills, could have been valuable to the British troops if arrangements for liaison between them had been established beforehand. As with many other defensive measures, the military planners had failed to arrange this. In the chaotic situation which developed after the invasion, the soldiers seldom asked the Volunteers for their advice about local conditions and, if given, it was not always taken.

When the Japanese landed near Kota Bharu in Kelantan on 8 December, Vincent Baker, Maurice's superior in the company and the manager of the Sungei Lembing tin mine, instructed him to organise the guarding of a jungle track which ran from Bandi, near Remanan in Trengganu to Machang, which formed part of the Kuala Reman estate. This track was not watched by the army or police and Vincent was worried that the invaders might use it to encircle Kuantan, which lies on the coast just to the south of the border between Trengganu and Pahang. Apart from arresting a number of Chinese using the track and sending them to the mine headquarters for questioning, three weeks passed without any sign of an enemy who had chosen the west side of the mountains, with its better road and rail facilities, as the main axis of advance down the peninsula.

The mine at Sungei Lembing and the town of Kuantan were undefended. Knowing that the Japanese would almost certainly occupy them, Vincent decided that, rather than seek safety in Singapore, he and his sister Nona would hide in the jungle until the British returned. Taking one of his Chinese managers, Cheng Kam, into his confidence, he had a refuge prepared near the jungle edge, stored it with food, and drew out enough money to pay for provisions for the months he expected that they would have to stay in hiding.

On 29 December the Japanese Takumi Detachment, sent south from Kota Bharu, was approaching Kuantan. That day the British Resident in Kuala Lipis instructed Vincent to destroy the mine, which was done the following morning by turning off the pumps and flooding the workings. The workers then threw the mined tin down the shaft to block it and deny the metal to the invader. Vincent was told to evacuate all Europeans without delay. Having many other things on his mind, not least paying off 6,000 workers who would now be out of a job, he was too busy to talk to Maurice Cotterill on the rubber estate, apart from letting him know that he was destroying the mine.

With no advice available from Vincent, Maurice went the next day to Kuantan. The District Officer confirmed that the Japanese were close and told Maurice to use his discretion in destroying transport, machinery, fuel, rubber, and other materials. Knowing that his employees, like the miners, would lose their jobs, Maurice went to the bank to draw cash for their wages. Finding that the bank had been evacuated to Gambang, he decided to drive there, which involved taking the ferry across the river. Because of an air raid, the ferry was not running and he had to turn back without any cash.

Some of the Europeans, by delaying their departure from Sungei Lembing, failed to pass through Kuantan before the Japanese occupied the town on the evening of 30 December. They left the next day in small parties on foot for Kuala Lipis, hoping to use a jungle track leading to Pohoi on the road between Kuantan and Jerantut, where they expected to find British troops. From there they planned to make their way to Singapore and so, they thought, to safety. The last party, seven men and one woman, left at five o'clock in the afternoon on New Year's Eve.

On 28 December, a British 'stay-behind' party under an officer from the Royal Corps of Signals, Major Roscher, and including a wireless operator called Chiang, had arrived in Kuantan seeking a suitable site in which to set up a radio transmitter. They asked Vincent to suggest two men with local knowledge who could move into the jungle when the Japanese came and man the station with Chiang. He said that Maurice and Brian Tyson would be suitable for the task. Also at his suggestion, a Sinhalese man called Fanseca, the chief electrician at the mine, agreed to act as their contact with the outside world while continuing to live and work in the open under the Japanese. We shall meet Fanseca, a man of exceptional courage, again. He was employed by the Japanese in running the electricity generating station in Kuantan and remained active in the resistance until late in the war, providing a news service to the community based on British and American broadcasts. When finally betrayed, he was tortured by his captors for a week until he died, refusing to the end to reveal where his set was hidden. It is through the courage of such people that evil is overcome.

On 31 December, with the Japanese in Kuantan, Vincent confirmed to Maurice that he should destroy all the plant and machinery on the rubber estate. Maurice apologised to the employees for his inability to pay them their wages. Instead he asked his overseers to hand out all the rice and other equipment in the stores, estimating that each worker would receive about 20 *gantangs* of rice. After overseeing the destruction of the machinery and the materials used in converting the latex, Maurice went to Vincent's bungalow at Sungei Lembing where the other remaining Europeans had gathered. Here he met Roscher and Chiang.

Roscher asked the men gathered in the bungalow for volunteers to stay behind and operate the radio transmitter from the jungle. Not knowing that Vincent had already nominated them, Maurice and Brian Tyson volunteered, along with a third man, James Watson Smith. After an emotional goodbye to their friends, Vincent and his sister Nona went to their hideout in the jungle, promising to be in touch with Maurice the next day. As they were leaving, looters were already busy in the bungalows vacated by the Europeans, and were only deterred from entering Vincent's bungalow when they discovered Roscher, Chiang, and the three volunteers still inside.

That evening Maurice, Tyson, and Chiang took a lorry-load of what Maurice describes as *barang* (Malay word for 'things' or 'stuff') to the jungle edge and spent the rest of the night shifting it away from the road. At ten o'clock the following night they returned to Vincent's bungalow. There they found Smith and Roscher had been joined by some Indian soldiers, a member of the MCS called Shepherd, and John Davis of the Malayan Police. Before they left for Kuala Lumpur, Shepherd and Smith promised to return with some arms and ammunition for Maurice, Tyson, Chiang, and any resistance fighters they might recruit. It is probable that Nona Baker knew of this proposal, which, as we will see, was to lead to a fruitless search by the guerrillas many months later. Smith also promised to repair their wireless which was able to transmit but was not receiving any signals.

John Davis was a man of outstanding resource and courage, and an important contributor to peace and freedom in Malaya and in Malaysia. Shepherd and Smith were unable to send the stay-behind party the arms they had promised and Davis was the only one of the party at the Bakers' bungalow that fateful 1 January 1942 to contact Maurice and his team with instructions as the military debacle unfolded. Later, as Singapore was falling, Davis arranged an escape route through Sumatra, allowing hundreds of refugees to reach Australia or Ceylon. We will come across him again when we look at the activities of Force 136, of which the British Special Air Service (SAS) regiment established a Malayan Section in Ceylon in July 1942, and again when the communist leader, Chin Peng, insisted that Davis should escort him when he met Tunku Abdul Rahman in December 1955. Davis had joined the Malayan Police in Pahang in 1931 and retired to Britain in 1961. At school one of his friends was Kim Philby, the traitor who sent many men and women to their death by betraying them to the Russians. There could be no greater contrast in terms of service and loyalty than that between Davis and Philby.

Maurice, Brian, Fanseca, and Chiang spent the night of 1 January 1942 moving more of their gear into the jungle. Over the next ten days, with Fanseca going back each evening to Kuantan, they built a hut and set up their wireless transmission station. Maurice and Fanseca also arranged a relay of messengers to bring them information about Japanese troop movements. Although Vincent and Nona Baker's hideout was not far away, they made no attempt to contact Maurice and he could not visit them because he did not know where they were hiding.

On 12 January, using his code name *Cherry*, Chiang started to send off a radio message. The transmission equipment then available was very different from the models developed later in the war, being so heavy that it had to be carried by two men. In addition, it needed power generated by a motor which proved so noisy that Maurice quickly shut it down for fear of detection. The next day, having fixed up a rudimentary silencer for the engine, Chiang succeeded in making a report, although they had little news to impart. Their second and final broadcast, on 15 January, was equally devoid of information as the Japanese were preventing all Chinese men leaving Kuantan and the courier information line had already broken down.

On 18 January two Chinese, Ah Gin and Ah Suan, accompanied by a Kong Foo guide, arrived from Davis with instructions for Brian and Chiang to break camp and make their way to Segamat, where they should report to the police station.

The messengers had been stopped on their way by Japanese soldiers but destroyed the written message before being searched. They hid the cumbersome wireless equipment, which they were clearly unable to take with them, and gave away to their helpers the provisions which they could carry. Next day they set off at dusk, having failed in a final attempt to get in touch with the Bakers. By then it had become important not to delay in moving away from the area of their camp, which rather too many local Chinese knew about and, having travelled a safe distance, they spent the rest of the night in an isolated Chinese house. A police detective from the Chinese province of Nylam and his friend were already hiding there and asked to join the new arrivals. Maurice agreed, so long as they carried some of the *barang*. It was a decision he later had cause to regret.

With their combat troops involved in the march on Singapore, it was not surprising that the Japanese did not have the resources to control the territory which they had so quickly and easily occupied. Off the main roads and outside the towns, European fugitives could travel on foot relatively freely, except for the possibility that their presence might be reported to the Japanese. On tracks in the jungle pedestrians have to put up with hazards such as leeches and prickly plants, which soon cause infected wounds. Because of the lack of sunlight on the forest floor even on a cloudless day, it is very hard for a stranger to travel in the right direction without a compass. The terrain of mountain range running down the peninsula is broken up by ridges and streams which hamper any progress and make travelling on the level in a straight line impossible. To leave a track and try to make your way through virgin jungle with a *parang* means not merely that you become lost but that you make virtually no progress. The only practicable way for the fugitives to travel and evade capture, as Maurice and his companions were to discover on their journey south, was to use the rivers.

On 20 January, the party travelled by day on a track to Sungei Pohoi, reaching the road between Kuantan and Jerantut shortly before dusk. The guide went forward to see if it was safe to cross the bridge over the river. He returned with the alarming, but almost certainly exaggerated, report that 300 Japanese were stationed on the bridge and that using the road was impossible. He advised the party to return to Sungei Lambing.

After a miserable and downcast night on the river bank, Maurice spent an hour trying to persuade the guide to seek an alternative route to Segamat. When that failed, he resorted to a more compelling argument in the form of $50, with a promise of a further $50 if the party arrived there safely. The guide left them again and, after being away all day, returned at five in the afternoon to report that the Japanese had gone. The party waited until dusk before crossing the bridge. During his absence, the guide had not been idle, having fashioned two primitive rafts on which they drifted down the Pohoi river for an hour before making camp on the river bank.

The following day, 22 January, the refugees continued to pole their way down the Pohoi and then the Sungei Lepar rivers. Due to the rudimentary nature of their rafts and their own lack of expertise, both the refugees and their goods frequently fell into the stream. As dusk fell, it started raining and the wretched men, tired and wet, were up much of the night trying to dry their clothes. They were also very hungry, having been on half rations since they left their original hideout. At dawn the next day, as they continued down the Sungei Lepar, Maurice was surprised to see a wild elephant cross the river about 20 yards ahead of his raft.

At eleven o'clock in the morning of 23 January, when they were approaching the Pahang river, three of the Chinese men went forward to see if it was safe to cross to the other side. They returned at dusk with Malays and two boats but warned that, because of other people on the river, the Europeans should only make the crossing under the cover of darkness. Safely across in the dark, some of the party passed a comfortable night in a Malay house, leaving Maurice, Brian, Chiang, and the guide to spend another disagreeable night on the river bank.

On 24 January the Malay boatmen carried the party up the Sungei Mentaga, arriving at around eleven in the morning at a house where they were given a wonderful feast of pork, and their first real meal since leaving their hideout. When their Chinese hosts said that they could take them to Kuala Keratong, they paid off the Malay boatmen. However, as soon as the Malays had left, the Chinese demanded $150 before they would act as guides. As Maurice, Brian and Chiang were by this time running short of cash, they refused to pay. The guide who had led them thus far did not knowwhich path to take but Ah Gin and Ah Suan said they knew the way and so the party departed, again making camp for the night in the jungle.

The next day, 25 January, they became completely lost. It had started to rain heavily and they could find no sign of any track. The original guide left to see if he could locate any

Sakais, as members of a tribe lived in the vicinity. He returned after nightfall with an old tribesman who took them to a house for the night. Next day other Sakais guided the party to the Sungei Aur river, which they reached at six o'clock in the evening. There, on 27 January, they obtained two Malay boats to travel downstream and at four o'clock in the afternoon reached Kuala Keratong, where they were warmly welcomed at his houseboat by Ah Fong, a contractor from Jelutong in Perak. With his help they were able to make arrangements for boats to take them up to Sungei Keratong.

Leaving at five o'clock in the morning, on 28 January, the party stayed all day on the river, arriving in the evening at the house of Ah Fong's brother, where they spent the night. Here they were able to find guides who promised to take them to Tumang, near Batu Enam, the next day. Having made an early start, the party reached the village of Palong at four o' clock in the afternoon. Chinese members of the party went ahead to see if it was safe to proceed and learned that the whole area was occupied by the Japanese. It then transpired that Ah Fong's brother had the previous day told some of his fellow Chinese that he had heard a rumour that Segamat was in Japanese hands. If this were so, as seemed probable, he had suggested giving them two bags of rice so that they could take refuge in the jungle. They only reported this conversation to Maurice when they realised that their escape route to the south had been closed. Unable to proceed further in safety, Brian and Chiang decided to return to Kuala Keratong and take up the offer Ah Fong's brother had made.

In the nine days since they left Kuantan, they had travelled the length of Pahang from north to south and had reached the boundary of Johore. However on 30 January they were back at Kuala Keratong, where they were again made welcome. The original guide said that he was confident of making his way to Singapore through the Japanese lines if he travelled alone. Having failed to deliver his charges to Segamat, he returned to Maurice the $50 which Maurice had advanced. Maurice and Tyson wrote notes for him to give to their employer's agents, The Borneo Company, explaining their position, and wished him good luck. The rest of the party went out to buy whatever provisions they could find to sustain them for what they feared would be a lengthy stay in the jungle.

The next day the refugees were shown an old Sakai site in the jungle where they could set up a permanent camp. Because the party was too large to remain concealed and be supplied with food, Maurice told the detective and his friend that the party would have to split up. To reduce the numbers further, Ah Gin volunteered to return to live in the local community as their outside contact. This would leave Ah Suan, Chiang, and the two Europeans in the camp. After 1 February had been spent assembling stores and making camp, their plans were again frustrated when Ah Fong's brother told them that the Sakai had become alarmed by the presence of Europeans in their territory. To avoid the risk of betrayal to the Japanese, the refugees decided to move further into the jungle.

On 2 February, as he was making preparations for his departure, the detective asked Maurice to exchange pistols with him. Because the heavier police pistol was a better weapon, Maurice agreed. They also decided that the three who were not remaining in the jungle would leave the next day. Before the parting, it was arranged that Chiang and Ah Suan, with the detective and his friend, would go to Kuala Keratong to buy up provisions as a reserve for the men staying behind. For this purpose, Chiang took with him the considerable sum of $100, which was the greater part of Maurice's remaining cash.

The following day at six o'clock in the morning, Ah Gin and Ah Suan arrived back at the camp with the news that the detective and his friend had murdered Chiang in their presence and that of Ah Fong's brother, and made off with the cash, his watch, and his other possessions. They all returned at once to the brother's house to find that Chiang had been buried and that the house was deserted. There they also learned that all the Sakais had moved out of the area. With their money stolen and their benefactor gone, Maurice and Brian, with Ah Gin and Au Suan, changed their plans yet again and resolved to attempt to make their way through Japanese lines to Singapore.

They left at once, trying but failing to find a decent path leading to the south. That evening they decided that, if they could not find a track, they would have to use the river. The following day, 4 February, Maurice and Ah Suan stayed behind to construct a raft while Brian and Ah Gin continued looking for a track. Night fell without any sign of Brian and Ah Gin returning. It transpired that they had again failed to find any track and had become hopelessly lost in the jungle. At ten o'clock in the morning, Maurice heard Brian calling and the party was reunited.

After these hazards, they realised that trying to reach Singapore was hopeless and decided to use the raft to return to Kuala Keratong where they could rely on help from Ah Fong. Before they reached their destination, however, they hailed a Chinese boat in which Leong Kee, a *towkay* from Gambi in Sungei Keratong, was on his way to the village with a servant to obtain supplies. After a long talk and possibly because he thought he would be shot if he refused, Leong Kee took them to his house, whence they dispatched a message to Ah Fong telling him of their predicament.

When Maurice asked Leong Kee if there was a suitable place in the jungle nearby for them to make camp, Leong Kee sent for a man called Soo Ann who was of mixed Chinese and Sakai parentage. On 6 February, when Leong Kee went to see Ah Fong with Maurice's letter, Soo Ann took the refugees into the jungle where they made camp. It was here, supplied by Leong Kee through Soo Ann, that Brian, Ah Gin, and Ah Suan were hiding when Singapore fell on 15 February 1942.

We last saw Vincent and Nona Baker as they left their bungalow to go into hiding at Sumgei Lembing. Vincent estimated that it would be between six weeks and six months before the British returned. Telling everyone that they were going to make their way to Kuala Lipis, instead they met Cheng Kam and drove to the jungle edge where Nona abandoned her car and moved into their hidden hut, which was only a 15-minute walk from the garden of their bungalow. Cheng Kam had enlisted the help of two other Chinese men, Wong Ng and Lau Siu, to assist him in supplying the Bakers. Judging that the hideout was uncomfortably close to the bungalows, the next day Vincent and Nona moved for safety to a less comfortable place deeper into the jungle. They do not seem to have made any effort to contact Maurice, even though Cheng Kam knew where his camp was and knew on the same day about the order from John Davis to find his way to Segamat.

The Japanese were slow to take possession of the Sungei Lembing mining complex and when they did so, they found that everything capable of being moved had been looted, including refrigerators for which there was no power Nona's car was not destroyed as planned, and appeared to have been appropriated by Cheng Kam for his own use. The Japanese secret police, the *Kempeitai*, were anxious to find Vincent and suspected Cheng Kam of helping him. After Cheng Kam had been taken in for questioning, his wives protested strongly at his continuing to put himself and his family at risk and they rightly warned him that it was only a matter of time before someone would threaten to betray him and the Bakers.

In a few short weeks after 8 December 1941, the masters had become the hunted. Their physiognomy made it impossible for Europeans to move freely among the general population. Unable to survive on their own in the jungle, their life as fugitives depended entirely on the help they received from other races who, with every act on the European's behalf or every omission to report where they were, put their own safety and those of their families at risk. It is not surprising that Maurice Cotterill and Nona Baker developed a deep admiration for the people of Malaya, and especially for those of Chinese descent without whom they would have died a lonely death in the jungle, and that this should have led to their being sympathetic even to those who resorted to an armed rebellion in 1948.

5

The Invasion

The Japanese occupation of Malaya accelerated the process whereby the peninsula changed from an aggregation of semi-independent states under colonial government into a unitary nation. The ease with which the British forces were defeated destroyed any illusion there may have been, among the other inhabitants, of an all-powerful white supremacy. The conversion of the managerial elite, and their *mems*, into a rabble of refugees, and their subsequent humiliation by the Japanese, demonstrated their personal fallibility. The disregard in their flight for the safety of non-Europeans often showed little nobility when it came to saving their own skins. The fall of Singapore marked the beginning of the end of the British Empire.

This is a story about the freedom of Maurice Cotterill and of the Malaysian nation. We have neither the space nor the inclination to recapitulate everything which happened in the peninsula in the winter of 1941/1942, between the downing by Japanese pilots shortly before midnight on 6 December of a British *Catalina* reconnaissance plane in the Gulf of Siam; and the surrender by General Percival in the Singapore Ford factory at Bukit Timah, to General Yamashita on 15 February 1942, not just of the impregnable naval base but also of 15,000 Australian, 35,000 British, 65,000 Indian, and 15,000 Malay troops. Yamashita had under his command no more than 60,000 front-line soldiers, but, with an ineffective counterpart in Percival and total control of the air and the sea, that proved enough. He had beaten by six days the capitulation date predicated before the war by the military planners in Tokyo.

Four scenes in the drama or tragedy directly affected Maurice and those living in Kuantan. The first was the Japanese landing at Kota Bharu in Kelantan on the east coast to the north of Pahang just after midnight on 8 December. The second was the sinking of the capital ships, the *Prince of Wales* and the *Repulse*, on 10 December. The third was the use of guerrilla tactics against the invaders by Spencer Chapman from the Singapore No. 101 Special Training School prior to 14 February. The fourth was the fall of Singapore, which closed any escape route for Maurice, the Bakers, Chapman, and others like them trapped in the jungles of Malaya.

The Japanese 25th Army given the task of conquering Malaya consisted of the 5th, the 18th, and the Imperial Guards Divisions. These units were over strength and were in addition supported by an efficient rear-echelon. To oppose them were the 11th Indian Division, stationed near the border with Thailand; the 9th Indian Division, on the west coast to the south of Kuala Lumpur; and the 8th Australian Division, in Johore. There were also lightly-armed units of the Malay Regiment and the Volunteers, composed of civilians of all races. The Japanese soldiers had been picked from the best of the operational units in China and Manchuria. They had years of battle experience and had undergone intensive training before the campaign. Their infantry was supported by tanks, of which the British had none.

Most of the troops facing the invaders were the converse of their opponents in terms of experience, selection, and training. The fine prewar Divisions of the Indian army had been dispatched to North Africa and the Middle East, to protect the Nile Delta and the oil fields. The new recruits sent to serve in Malaya were for the most part young, untrained in jungle fighting, and often led by junior British officers not yet fluent in Urdu and so unable to communicate with their men. The one unit to have received thorough preparation for jungle warfare was a Scottish Battalion of the Argylls. The Australians, under General Gordon Bennett, had arrived in Malaya on 15 August 1941. They did little relevant training, either before or after the invasion, discouraged perhaps by a fine of £5 for every rubber tree they damaged. They, like the Argylls, were eventually proved doughty opponents of the Japanese when they were sent into action after the Japanese had overwhelmed the 11th Indian Division at Slim River on 7 January 1942.

It seems that the only person who thought the Japanese were not about to invade Malaya was the British Commander-in-Chief, Air Chief Marshal Sir Robert Brooke-Popham. It might have been no more than an attempt to maintain morale if he had announced publicly on 6 December, 'You can take it from me that there will be no Japanese bomb dropped on Singapore and there will never be a Japanese foot set in Malaya'. As he said it in private to his cipher clerk, he obviously believed it. He and Percival, his senior General, knew that an attack was likely to start with a landing in Thailand. The staff had prepared a plan called Operation Matador which involved making a pre-emptive move over the northern border, but it was not implemented. As a result the Japanese were unopposed when their boats arrived with troops and armour at Singora and Pattani, whence they commanded a direct invasion route into the states of Kedah and Perak, bypassing Perlis and Penang on the road to the south.

Unaware that the Japanese had already built an airfield at Phuket and provisioned four landing strips in Southern Thailand, the British saw that the obvious destination for a landing in Malaya was Kota Bharu, in northern Kelantan, where there was a fine airfield just inland from the sandy beaches. A railway wound its way south from the town through the hills and valleys to Kuala Lipis, but there was no highway along the east coast to the town of Kuantan. If Kota Bharu were lost, the other two airfields in northern Malaya at Gong Kedah and Machang would also be untenable. Nor might it be possible to protect those at Alor Star, Sungei Patani, and Butterworth. It was therefore crucial to oppose any landings at Kota Bharu.

As control of the air was to play a decisive part in the conflict, it may help to compare the planes available to the combatants. Of the 134 serviceable aircraft available to the British, 84 were provided by Australia and New Zealand, including 60 obsolete *Brewster Buffalo* fighter planes, of which three were based at Kota Bharu together with *Hudson* bombers. In addition, the Royal Air Force deployed 47 bombers and 3 reconnaissance *Catalinas*, including the one which was shot down before the war started. The invaders deployed 152 modern fighters, 130 bombers, and over 50 reconnaissance aircraft, all of them to a higher specification than their opponents, and with more experienced crews.

The Australian airmen at Kota Bharu knew early in December that a Japanese convoy was sailing towards the Gulf of Siam but the low cloud of the monsoon stopped the

Hudson crews tracking it. In any event they were forbidden to attack before a ship came within the three-mile territorial limit for fear of causing a diplomatic incident.

At 12.25 a.m. on 8 December, the first landing craft hit the beach at an islet in the mouth of the river close to Kota Bharu town, followed by fresh waves of troops at two-hour intervals. From dawn that day, Japanese planes attacked all the northern airfields. In just three of them, they destroyed 60 out of 100 planes on the ground, while in the air the *Buffalo* proved no match for the *Zero*. By the evening of the first day, there was no longer any air cover for the defending troops and within a week the Japanese had won total control of the skies above Malaya.

The task of protecting the three northerly airfields and opposing a landing on the long sandy beaches of Kelantan had been entrusted to the 4,000 men of the 8th Indian Infantry Brigade which had arrived in Singapore under the command of Brigadier Berthold Key in October 1940. He guessed rightly where the landings would be made and erected beach defences which included two double apron wire fences as well as a coil of Dannert wire. Behind these obstacles were an interlocking series of pillboxes manned by soldiers with Bren guns and hand-grenades. The beaches were also mined. Apart from his Brigade, he had under command a Company of the Malay Regiment and elements of the Pahang and Perak Volunteers. His artillery consisted of three batteries amounting to 16 18-pounder field guns and eight 2-pounder anti-tank guns but no armoured vehicles. The 18-pounder guns with split trails were veterans from World War I, and would have been more effective converted to 25-pounders. The 2-pounders were of small value.

The assault troops at Kota Bharu numbered 5,590. Because of the monsoon, the surf was running up to ten feet, creating difficulty in getting into the landing craft from the ships as well as a hazardous trip to the beach. Some 1,200 Japanese soldiers were to be posted as missing, the majority due to drowning, against 320 killed and 538 wounded in the subsequent fighting. The defenders sank 16 of the 48 landing craft and they, or the bombers, also sank the ship carrying the heavy armour. The men in the pillboxes discovered however that the .303 bullets fired by the Bren guns did not penetrate the iron hulls of the landing craft. A light shone out to sea by a Japanese agent, possibly the airfield barber/Major, guided the assault parties to the beach. The troops also came supplied with exact details of the location and nature of the defences they would face, and with the equipment to overcome them.

Despite their inexperience and lack of air support, the Indian infantry fought with great gallantry. With the pillboxes overcome and the defenders on the beaches surrounded, the Japanese occupied the town of Kota Bharu, from which expatriate civilians had fled, leaving those of other races to fend for themselves. Late on that fateful 8 December a message was sent to Singapore stating that the airfield was under attack. Brooke-Popham and Percival's response was an ominous portent. Without checking the veracity of the report, or its source, or speaking to the Commanding Officer, Wing Commander Noble, or to Brigadier Key, they ordered the evacuation of the airfield. When Key arrived in person to arrange the dispositions for his troops to defend the airfield, he found that it had already been abandoned, and no Japanese. The remaining five serviceable *Hudson* bombers fled to safety in Kuantan, evading prowling *Zero* fighters by flying so low above the beaches that the palm trees gave them cover. Within hours the airfield was being used by the Japanese.

On 12 December, when it had become clear that the Japanese thrust would be down the western plain, Percival ordered Key to evacuate Kelantan. The tortuous railway line from Kuala Krai, with its bridges and cuttings, was Key's only route south. If that were cut by the Japanese, his Brigade would be isolated. However, by withdrawing the 8th Indian Brigade, which was unbeaten and had suffered comparatively few casualties, Percival committed an error of generalship. It was not just that he ceded territory and freed a greater number of Japanese to join the main thrust against the 11th Indian Division. At the very start of the conflict, he had conceded moral supremacy to the invader as he was to do on other occasions when, through ordering a retreat rather than resistance, he destroyed the fighting spirit of his troops.

Key withdrew his men and most of his equipment by rail without loss or pressure on his rearguard, destroying bridges as they passed, including the great five-span Guillemard viaduct. The Japanese did not reopen the line and used the metals for the construction of their infamous railway from Saigon to Rangoon. Following the British withdrawal, most of the Japanese troops from Kelantan joined the attackers on the west coast. Others, the Takumi Detachment, took the tracks along the east coast through Trengganu to Kuantan, which, as we saw, they reached on 30 December 1941.

Thus not only did the British lose command of the air but their High Command squandered its resources including the most important of all, the fighting spirit of their Indian soldiers. Kota Bharu was not lost through the incompetence or cowardice of Brigadier Key and his men. Nor was it to be through incompetence or cowardice that the command of the sea was lost.

Churchill had used the *Prince of Wales* for his conference with President Roosevelt in August 1941. Alive to the threat to Malaya, and its denuded defences, against the advice of his admirals he insisted on sending his most modern and powerful battleship to Singapore. Air cover was to be provided by the new carrier *Indomitable*. When the carrier ran aground on its shake-down trials, Churchill sent in its place the battle cruiser *Repulse*. The two capital ships arrived in Singapore on 2 December 1941. The Japanese staff at Imperial Headquarters were alarmed by this threat to their convoys on the long voyage from Hainan to the invasion ports and beaches. Knowing the formidable anti-aircraft defences at the naval base, they wondered how they might entice the capital ships into the open sea where they could be attacked with bombs and torpedoes. Their dilemma was solved when, on 8 December, their agents told them that the ships had left port at dusk. Hirohito, who had been following the Kelantan landings on short-wave radio, told his commanders that every available aircraft must be diverted to the search for the British fleet and its destruction was to take priority over any other mission.

It was ironic that Admiral Tom Phillips, commanding the fleet of two capital ships and four destroyers, should have been a strong advocate of building aircraft carriers rather than battleships. He, as well as anyone, knew the risk he was taking in seeking out the Japanese convoys without air cover. For two days, aided by the monsoon clouds and good seamanship, his fleet evaded detection from the air. To cause further confusion, on 9 December, he sent the *Tenedos*, the oldest escorting destroyer, back towards Singapore as a decoy, with instructions to broadcast radio signals as if from himself.

On 10 December, learning of the evacuation of the airfield at Kota Bharu, Phillips knew that his mission had failed. He was then off Kuantan and sent a destroyer, the *Express*, into the harbour to check the situation in the town. Finding it quiet, he decided to creep up the coast in the hope of surprising the transports and naval vessels still lying off Kota Bharu. At 11.15 a.m., his luck ran out when the weather cleared and his ships were spotted by a Japanese plane.

Phillips knew that his only chance of survival was in the open sea, where his ships could take evasive action against torpedo attacks. With its 95-barrel machine cannons and 32 pom-pom anti-aircraft guns, the *Prince of Wales* was able to fire 60,000 projectiles a minute. That might have been considered enough to beat off air attacks for the seven hours he needed before reaching the safety of Singapore through the darkness. Unfortunately, as with the Americans, the British had no conception of the quality of the enemy aircraft and the skill of Japanese pilots. All the Japanese needed were three hours. Their losses were three planes. The British lost both capital ships, 840 men, and command of the sea.

Phillips refused to leave his ship and returned to the bridge as the *Prince ofWales* went down. He had known the gamble he had taken in his attempt to disrupt the landings. Twice his fleet had come close to achieving surprise off the beachheads, and had had to withdraw. Unlike those at Pearl Harbor, his great battleship died in the ocean fighting rather than tied up at a quayside. The Japanese pilots, whether through gallantry or a shortage of ammunition, allowed the three destroyers to pick up survivors. A plane dropped a message on the *Vampire* which read 'We have completed our task; you may carry on.' In Tokyo, hearing the news by phone, Marquis Kido, the Lord Privy Seal, shouted out in English 'Hip, hip, hooray!' From that day on, Japanese troop convoys heading south through the islands towards Australia would be immune from naval attack.

Spencer Chapman's exploits in the fortnight before the fall of Singapore are relevant because they revealed the problems of concealment facing Europeans behind enemy lines, the opportunities Malay topography afforded for guerrilla warfare, and the possibility of concealment in the jungle. It may be unfortunate that we have to rely entirely on the story he tells in his classic book *The Jungle is Neutral*. Maurice Cotterill's dislike of Chapman arose in part because he considered him a braggart. Nona Baker, who admired Chapman, noted that in his few references to her and her bother Vincent in the book, there were three errors of fact. But, even if the exploits may have been somewhat exaggerated, the basic premises remain valid.

On 22 December 1941, Chapman arrived in Kuala Lumpur from Singapore where, you may recall, he had been Second-in-Command of No. 101 Special Training School instructing stay-behind parties in the arts of guerrilla warfare. His first mission was to go behind Japanese lines and report on their numbers, transport, equipment, and morale. He was also asked to observe what help the local inhabitants were providing to the invader. Crossing the Perak river, he spent several days moving in the vicinity of Kuala Kangsar and Batu Gajah before returning to report at Teluk Anson to General Anson, commanding the 11th Indian Division. Chapman was convinced that, in the military vacuum behind the Japanese forward troops, a small force could cause havoc and asked the General to give him 500 men. Putting his hand on Chapman's shoulder, Anson told him he was so short of men that he could not afford to release ten, or even one; this while the Australian 8th Division was still mounting guard against non-existent saboteurs and avoiding damaging rubber trees in its camps in Johore.

Chapman then set about collecting stores and munitions which were carried into a jungle cache by Chinese helpers with help from some Malays working under a Sikh foreman. Perhaps inevitably, thieves were told the location of this horde, with each nationality blaming the others for the betrayal. Hearing explosions from nearby on 13 January Chapman found that the store had been looted and the money left there had been stolen. Fortified perhaps by some whisky, the robbers had celebrated by setting off some of the explosives which enabled Chapman's team to locate them and recover much of the food and explosives, although their failure to find the detonators caused problems in the days ahead. The cash and the whisky were not recovered.

Other 'stay-behind' parties did not start operating before Singapore fell. The British knew that Europeans would not be able to move freely in occupied territory and they were told to escape to Sumatra rather than remain in hiding. A party established by Chapman, led by a Volunteer rubber planter called Frank Vanrenan, also had its concealed supplies stolen. After various adventures, they were executed by the Japanese. Thus, at the beginning of February 1942 there remained only one trained body, consisting of Chapman, another British soldier called John Sartin, and Bill Harvey, a rubber planter in the Volunteers, to harass the lines of communication of the three Japanese Divisions converging on Singapore.

Chapman and his team started sabotaging the railway line and attacking motor vehicles on the main highway on 1 February. They were fed and sheltered by Chinese sympathisers who warned them that any European spotted by a Tamil or a Malay, or even by a Chinese stranger, was in danger of being reported to the Japanese. Disguised as Tamils, they left their hideout in the jungle each night to blow up the railway line, to derail trains, to lay charges on the highway, and on two occasions to ambush a military convoy. At the outset, the Japanese were using both the road and the railway throughout the night, their vehicles driving with their lights on, having no fear of air attack. Many of the troops were on bicycles and Chapman soon realised that cyclists who tied their weapons to the frame were easy game because they took too long to free them when they were ambushed. They found the railway, on which retreating British had destroyed only half the locomotives, to be fully operational and totally unguarded. They were also to discover that the Japanese soldier enjoyed being shot at in the dark from the jungle no more than the British, and, like the British, would waste hundreds of rounds, despite having no target to aim at, rather than pursue an attacker through the undergrowth.

Two weeks later, when Singapore fell and continuing operations would only bring down reprisals on civilians, Chapman, Sartin, and Harvey called a halt. Using records available after the war, Chapman claimed that they had derailed 7 or 8 trains, damaged 15 railway bridges, cut the line in about 60 places, destroyed up to 40 motor vehicles, and killed or wounded between 500 and 1,500 men. They had forced the Japanese to place sentries and establish patrols along the railway and the highway, and to abandon using them at night. Two thousand soldiers needed for the assault on Singapore had been withdrawn to Tanjung Malim and Kuala Kubu to track them down. All this was achieved by three men, with local support from courageous Chinese helpers.

The British High Command knew that the invasion would probably come through Thailand. Having drawn back from making a pre-emptive strike north, they had in Penang a force of 500 Indian Volunteers along with other military personnel. These men were in a position to threaten the Japanese lines of communication as their army advanced south, and could have been reinforced from Singapore. Instead of using this weapon, Europeans, military and civilian, abandoned Penang without a fight, leaving the Indian Volunteers to surrender and a Sinhalese man the task of lowering the Union Jack when the conquerors arrived. The British did not even pause to sink the flotilla of small boats which the invaders were able to use in their leapfrog landings behind British lines down the coast. At least in 1945 the Royal Marines had the good manners to give the task of raising the Union Jack to the Sinhalese again.

By the time the Japanese forces reached the tip of the peninsula facing Singapore, 20,000 Indian troops had surrendered and the majority of the others had no stomach for the fight. When finally committed, the Australians found that they could exchange their obsolete rifles with more modern weapons thrown down by Indian troops they called the 'Galloping Gwalis'. The Australians outfought and inflicted heavy losses on Yamashita's men, who were no longer fresh after their epic advance. A single Division, even a Division of Australians, was not enough to hold the entire front, even supported by the Leicesters, the Ghurkas, and the 90 surviving Argylls. On 23 January, Percival decided that he must withdraw all his forces on to the island. After the last of the retreating troops had passed, part of the 70-foot wide causeway joining the island to Malaya was dynamited. Clearly Percival did not contemplate that his army would need it to reconquer Malaya.

Singapore is the size of the Isle of Wight and much the same shape. (It was symptomatic of the chaos that during the battle for the island the Intelligence Corps issued extra 50 maps to a British unit, who had been limited to one map for the entire Battalion. Unfortunately they were of the Isle of Wight, not of Singapore.) Even though it would have been prudent and easy to do so before the war, Percival had decided not to prepare defences on the north shore facing Malaya on the ground that it would have been bad for morale. In the four days before the assault boats landed, searchlights were placed to illuminate the beaches, and his men dug slit trenches. No effective efforts were made, however, to establish defensive machine-gun posts or to cover the shore. It was not as if the British lacked men or matériel. The Japanese were to capture in the city enough fuel, food, and ammunition to supply their campaign in the Pacific islands for weeks.

On 9 February soldiers from the Japanese 5th and 18th Divisions crossed the short strait between the peninsula and the island and established a beachhead. By dusk on 12 February the attackers had taken the high ground at Bukit Timah and threatened the city's reservoirs. The flow of water from Johore had been severed when the causeway was blown up and the supply of potable water became critical when the defenders killed and wounded Japanese soldiers bathing in the Peirce Reservoir, which flowed into the Seletar, rendering both undrinkable. Three other reservoirs remained operational but Japanese shelling had ruptured many water mains although it was not until the afternoon of 15 February that the supply failed completely.

In the confusion the British command structure collapsed. Individual units fought with great gallantry, and none more so that the Chinese, both Volunteers and communists, fighting in Dalforce under Colonel John Dalley and flying the Chinese flag. The Japanese directed their accurate artillery fire from the observatory belonging to the Sultan of Johore which gave a commanding view of the island as well as the heavens, and used his residence as Headquarters, confident that the British would not wish to upset their host by damaging his property. They made short work of the few *Spitfires* sent to defend the city.

A critical event, psychologically, occurred when forces under Colonel Tsuji captured the Alexandra Barracks Hospital and killed with bayonets 230 patients and 93 members of the staff, releasing the others to tell the British what would happen throughout the city if there were no surrender. The two junior officers who ordered the massacre were subsequently tried and executed by the Japanese, but this example of terror, which had not intimidated Chiang Kai-shek in Nanking, influenced Percival's decision that further resistance was futile. The population of the city, swollen with refugees to over a million, included thousands of European civilians whose lives he did not wish to put at risk.

Yamashita claimed subsequently that his attack on Singapore had been a bluff. His men had fought their way south for over 500 miles and were suffering from disease as well as combat. He was short of both food and ammunition. He faced an enemy with vastly greater resources in terms of men and matériel. He realised that the outcome of the fight for the city had been finely balanced on 12 February and Percival's failure of nerve two days later surprised him.

The British make various excuses for their defeat, some of which are unconvincing. An Allied Conference on the defence of Malaya held in 1940 had suggested that protecting the frontier with Thailand would need 40 Battalions, including armoured vehicles, and 566 modern aircraft. Percival had 32 Battalions in all under command, he had no tanks, and the aircraft were obsolescent and few in number. We have seen how he frittered away his resources by ordering retreat and by committing units to battle piecemeal, like putting paper though a shredder. The coastal defence guns defending the base pointed seawards, but would have been of little use against infantry landing in small boats.

The suggestion by Percival and by General Wavell, who took over after the incompetent Brooke-Popham was removed on 23 December 1941, that the invaders had the help of fifth-columnists, is unsubstantiated. There were very few Chinese who welcomed the Japanese and most Malays and Indian civilians were no more than hapless spectators. Yamashita did not need local help. He had with him many of the 4,000 or more Japanese who knew the country well and had left it only a month before the invasion. In all the circumstances, the continued loyalty to the British of Malays as well as Chinese is remarkable. After Singapore fell, the Japanese executed 100 men of the Malay Regiment because they refused to renounce their former allegiance, and not one Gurkha joined the Indian National Army. The Australian commander deserted his troops before the surrender. Thereafter running shoes were known in his homeland as Gordon Bennetts.

Nona Baker guessed that Singapore had fallen when she saw a *Zero* doing a victory roll. Chapman was told the news by his Chinese protectors. Maurice Cotterill did not find out for some weeks. They then knew that they would now have to stay in the jungle until the British returned.

6

Joining the Guerrillas

Maurice Cotterill was hiding in the jungle with Brian Tyson, Ah Gin, and Ah Suan when Singapore fell, although the information did not reach him until April 1942, and even then he refused to believe it, thinking it was another rumour among the many which abounded in the absence of reliable news. We last saw them in a camp near Kuala Keratong where they were being fed by Leong Kee, the man they had hailed on the river, with Soo Ann acting as a messenger. Here they enjoyed luxuries such as sleeping mats, pillows, and plates, although it rained at night and their hut leaked. Soo Ann visited the camp every four or five days, bringing rice and fish, with occasional luxuries such as pork, sugar, or flour.

The speed of their conquest meant that there was a pause before the Japanese took control of outlying districts. In the cities and towns, however, they acted at once to cow the population, and especially the Chinese, by carrying out arbitrary executions. In Singapore, Penang, Taiping, and other places they left the heads of decapitated victims on display as a warning to others. In the month of February 1942 between 5,000 and 7,000 Chinese were massacred in Singapore alone, and members of the Malay Regiment who refused to swear allegiance to the new masters were used by the troops for bayonet practice. Failure by any passer-by to bow to a private soldier on sentry duty was judged to be an insult to the Emperor and led to a beating or worse.

In every town Chinese men were subject to 'screening', a

process resulting in the arbitrary imprisonment or killing of anyone who, in the judgment of the secret police, the dreaded *Kempeitai*, might challenge Japanese rule. The *Kempeitai* were not subject to the rule of law or military discipline and army commanders were powerless to prevent their excesses even had they chosen to do so. As early as 20 December 1941 the Chinese residents of Pasir Puteh in Kelantan had been ordered to attend the police station and five men had been executed for failing to give information about the account books of the local branch of the China Relief Fund. In George Town, on the island of Penang, and in other towns, masked informers denounced their victims. Many innocent men were killed and thousands were sent to prison, usually for a short stay. Besides targeting the Chinese especially, proclamations on posters and in the newspapers uttered dire threats to those of any race who did not accept Japanese rule. A person helping fugitive Europeans put not merely his own life at risk: he exposed his family and community to retribution. An informer, on the other hand, could expect a substantial reward, although not to inform could also be a capital offence.

On 12 March, Leong Kee decided that too many people knew that there were Europeans hiding nearby and that Maurice and Brian, with their two Chinese companions, must move to a more remote camp. To prevent further gossip, he told people that the party had returned to Sungei Lembing. Soo Ann built a shelter for them deeper in the jungle, which they were delighted to discover had a roof which didn't leak. The jungle is generous with its building materials, atap palm leaves for the roof and walls, rattan for the binding material, a stout tree to support the structure, and green timber or bamboo for the frame. In the jungle there is also plenty of water, but it provides no food apart from fish in the rivers, animals to shoot, or possibly wild fruit in season. As Maurice and his companions had no rifles, and would not have dared to use them if they had, nor any fishing gear, they were entirely dependent for survival on Leong Kee's courage and generosity, and on Soo Ann's visits.

The *orang asli*, the descendants of the original inhabitants of the peninsula who inhabit the jungle, hunt with blowpipes and cultivate crops in their clearings. As one of their main harvests is tapioca, which makes the ground infertile, they have to shift camp on a regular basis. Not unnaturally, their jungle lore is acute and, when the British buried supplies, the tribesmen invariably detected the cache, whether of food, weapons, or diaries, as all the fugitives were to discover. They also knew all the tracks and clearings in the jungle, and they were formidable trackers. In the dark days of April 1942, nobody could be certain whether they would remain quiet about the presence of Europeans in their territory.

As early as December 1941, young Chinese men and women in Perak had taken to the jungle to avoid interrogation or capture by the Japanese. Before the MPAJA and other guerrilla bands had established regular support systems among the kampongs, they obtained supplies by making forays from their hideouts and demanding food and money from *towkays*, or Chinese merchants. In March one such gang in the jungle near Kuala Keratong descended on Ah Fong, Maurice's first benefactor. The raid frightened Leong Kee, who demanded that the refugees move away from his area. He also told them that he could no longer go on feeding them.

Two days later, on 30 March, Maurice, Tyson, and their Chinese companions decided with great reluctance that their party was too large to feed and that they must separate. Ah Gin and Ah Suan left to rejoin their community, with a strict injunction from the Europeans to rejoin them if they found themselves in any danger. All four men were deeply affected by the parting. They had gone through much together and formed a close bond. They split their remaining cash four ways, each being left with $20.

As soon as the Chinese had left, although Tyson was unwell from ulcers on his legs which were so deep that he could scarcely walk, he and Maurice moved deeper into the jungle where they built a temporary shelter. They stayed there for ten days, a period during which Maurice only mentions in his diary a shortage of tobacco and of matches. In an era when everyone smoked, the Bakers and Chapman were also to deplore the absence of tobacco during their jungle years. It would not be long before the entire population of Malaya was to run out of matches.

On 10 April 1942, being short of food, Maurice returned with Tyson to Keratong where Leong Kee received them warmly, gave them their first square meal for many days, and seemed to have recovered his nerve, although he was anxious for the safety of his possessions with the Chinese guerrillas still in the area. He had transferred his stores into the jungle, using a hut which was only three-quarters of a mile from his house, and suggested that the two Europeans should move there and act as guards. Nine days later, on 19 April, a Sakai picked up the track to the hut and Leong Kee said that they must move at once. Soo Ann then took them five miles further into the jungle where he built them another shelter.

It was ten days before Soo Ann reappeared, during which the fugitives had nothing to eat other than rice, and that was running low. They saw plenty of fish in the stream but had no means of catching them. Sharing their anxiety about food, Soo Ann took them to see Leong Kee, who stocked them up with provisions and gave them some fishing tackle. This time they took the precaution of marking the track so that they would know in future how to get out of the jungle without a guide.

For the next month they spent much of their time fishing, which improved their diet, and made weekly visits to Leong Kee. Although they were no longer short of food, Tyson contracted beri-beri, a complaint caused by a shortage of vitamin B, of which a symptom is a swelling of the limbs. This was a condition from which all the fugitives suffered at one time or another, and became endemic among the prisoners of war sent to work on the Burma railway. Maurice, in his diary, writing with concern for his companion's health, expressed the hope that help, in the form of a British return, would not be long delayed. Three long years were to pass before that help arrived.

The *orang asli* obviously knew where the refugees were hiding and on 26 March a Sakai came to the hut to tell them that robbers had gone to Leong Kee's house, resulting in much rifle fire. Anxious about their friend's safety, Maurice and Tyson went to investigate and found him in the best of spirits. The 'robbers' were in fact guerrillas, probably the same as those that had visited Ah Fong a few weeks earlier, and they had taken goods only to the value of $300. More importantly, they had invited Maurice and Tyson, through Leong Kee, to join them.

This offered the prospect of a safer refuge for them without continuing to endanger their loyal Chinese friends and Maurice agreed to meet them with Leong Kee, at a place about five miles away, which was too far for the sick Brian Tyson to travel.

After meeting the leader of the guerrillas with Leong Kee on 2 June 1942, Maurice agreed to join them. He gave Leong Kee a note exonerating him from any responsibility should things turn out badly. Because there were Japanese in the vicinity, Maurice had to wait until dusk before being guided to the guerrilla camp. In the dark he fell from a rattan bridge and broke his wrist as well as causing a wound in his arm. He arrived in the camp at one in the morning. on 3 June and received a warm reception. The group had 30 members whose arms consisted of eight rifles and one tommy gun, to which were added his and Tyson's pistols.

Maurice's dairy entry reads, 'Chinese very good to me. I am laid up with bad arm and have to be fed.' Not only had he broken his wrist, an injury which weakened his arm for the rest of his life: he also contracted gangrene in the wound, which, in the absence of other medicine, the guerrillas cured by burning out the rotting flesh with acid. On 29 June 1942 Brian Tyson, still far from well, rejoined him.

Having seen Maurice and Tyson safely in the hands of guerrillas, we need to take a step back and record how Vincent and Nona Baker were faring.

The Bakers had been able to remain in comparative comfort close to Sumgei Lembing, regularly supplied with food brought to them by the three Chinese men, Cheng Kam, Wong Ng, and Lau Siu. They avoided malaria by sleeping under mosquito nets and they were supplied with quinine, which, along with all western medicines, was to become almost unobtainable for the civilian population as the occupation continued. They had taken with them into the jungle some $8,000 in cash and were able to pay their helpers $600 a month, of which Cheng Kam, who bought the food, kept half for himself. The Japanese continued to honour the colonial currency, the Straits dollar, supplementing it first with notes issued by the military, and then with occupation dollars, the 'banana' currency, so named from the motif on some notes. Although each of the dollars, including those without numbers, was declared to have the same value, the notes printed by the Japanese, lacking any backing, later moved to a discount and were declared worthless when the British returned. The Straits dollars, of which there remained very few in circulation, became the only legal tender after the occupation ended in 1945.

Nona Baker's suspicion, after seeing the victory roll, that Singapore had fallen was confirmed on 17 February through Fanseca's hidden radio. The Japanese occupied Sungei Lembing on 3 March, using Vincent's house as the residence for the commanding officer. After recovering the looted furniture, silver, and glass, the Japanese officer dined in state each evening, flavouring his dishes with his favourite condiment, tomato sauce, and waited on by Chinese house servants who had been trained by the British. The Japanese flag, or 'poached egg', now flew at Vincent's flagpole.

As the months passed, food became ever more difficult for Cheng Kam to procure. Even though his second wife was suffering from malnutrition, he and his two carriers continued to supply the Bakers. In an attempt to avert suspicion, they combined their trips to the jungle with the gathering of wood, an excuse which wore thin when Cheng Kam was given a post of minor responsibility by the Japanese. With many informers about, they found it necessary to reduce their visits, the interval between them sometimes reaching ten days. Even then too many people knew what was going on and it is an indication of the respect in which his employees held Vincent that it was not until 28 February 1943, when they had been more than a year in hiding, that they were threatened with exposure.

Nona and Vincent had heard from Cheng Kam about the communist guerrillas living in the Pahang jungle. Although communism was anathema to him, Vincent admired their courage and applauded their continued fight against the Japanese. When Lau Siu and Wong Ng told him that one of the gardeners on the plantation had threatened to tell the Japanese that they, with Cheng Kam, were supporting the fugitives unless he were paid a large sum in Straits dollars, Vincent knew they had to move. He refused to be blackmailed and said that he and Nona would join the o*rang-bukit* (hill people) which was the term used for the guerrillas. For their part, the communists already knew all about Vincent's refuge. They were anxious that he should join them, partly to gain kudos should the British return and partly because, by safeguarding him, they could demand regular subventions from the *towkays* in Kelantan, who had a similar interest in keeping all options open.

Lau Siu, Wong Ng, and another man who came to help carry their possessions, led the Bakers from their hut along a clear path through the jungle for two hours. After giving a sentry the password when they reached the camp, they were warmly welcomed by the guerrilla leader, Lao Lui, who, unlike some of the band, was a dedicated communist. Among his new colleagues Vincent was amused to discover the agitator whom he had sent packing from the mine before the war. Both he and Nona were delighted to find in the camp several men they already knew, including a fluent speaker of English called Reg Lawther, who had an Australian father and a Chinese mother. He, like all those who had worked in the mine, had great respect for Vincent. Only one person in the camp seemed to take pleasure in the humiliation of the *tuan besar*, or Head Man, which, as we shall see, was to have fatal consequences.

Lau Siu and Wong Ng shared a meal of tapioca and fish with the Bakers and Lao Lui, and they implored him to take good care of their new recruits. When they left, Vincent offered them the balance of their money, which they refused to accept, saying that they had been well paid already, and in any case would have done the same without payment. Nona was especially sorry to see their loyal and brave friends leave. Henceforth she became Pai Naa, or white Nona, while Vincent was no longer the tuan besar but Pai Ker, the indomitable one.

But before we go any further into their adventures with the MPAJA, we need to trace Spencer Chapman's route into the world of the guerrillas.

When they suspended operations against the Japanese·on the fall of Singapore, Chapman and his two companions were exhausted and they decided to lie low for a while in the jungle well away from Tanjung Malim and regain their strength before making their way to the coast and crossing the Straits of Malacca to Sumatra and, they supposed, safety. It might seem, in retrospect, an unwise decision because the longer they delayed their move, the tighter would be the control the Japanese obtained over the countryside. By moving far inland they also increased the risk of detection crossing the populated coastal plain on their way to the sea. In the first days of the occupation the Japanese did not patrol the minor roads nor had the police been organised to work for their new masters. By the time Chapman decided to make a move, it had already become suicidal for any European to be seen during daylight outside the jungle and dangerous to move during the nightly curfew.

Chapman seems also to have underestimated the risk of detection in other ways. On 22 February he and his companions, in broad daylight, were using explosives to stun fish. As they splashed about in the river naked collecting their catch, two men appeared on the bank and it was good fortune that the newcomers happened to be members of another British 'stay behind' party led by Pat Garden, which had established itself in the jungle a few miles northwest of Karak but had never started operating against the Japanese. They agreed to join forces but, because Garden had cut his hand badly with a parang, they delayed their move to join the rest of his party for three days. Among Garden's party was a middle-aged rubber planter called Chrystal who, despite suffering from duodenal ulcers, was to become one of the small band of European refugees to survive in the jungle until the end of the war.

Chapman describes in his book the series of disasters which attended their attempt to reach the coast riding bicycles at night along metalled roads. When they set off on 8 March, the party split into two. Chapman and his two companions managed to pass through Kuala Kubu and Kelumpang safely but it became clear that they had no hope of avoiding detection if they continued to Tanjung Malim. They decided to seek refuge again with Leu Kim, who had provided food and shelter for Chapman and his team during their operations in the area at the beginning of February. They then discovered that an informer had betrayed Leu Kim to the Japanese, who had burned down his house.

The entire area had been punished by the Japanese for the havoc wrought by Chapman's team early in February. Stung by their losses and their failure to catch the perpetrators, the Japanese had acted with extreme brutality to all the Chinese in the area, and in one atrocity had driven over 100 men, women, and children into an atap shed and burned them alive. It is not surprising that Chapman found ready helpers among the Chinese community even though it was he and his party who had stirred up the hornet's nest in the first place.

The Chinese reported that the guerrillas were well organised locally and Chapman wrote them a letter, telling him that he had been the commander of the Special Training School in Singapore (which he had not been) and requesting a meeting. In due course an English-speaking envoy called Chin Peng, later to lead the communists in the uprising, appeared and before long Chapman and his companion, a keen yachtsman called Haywood, were taken to the Ulu Slim camp where they were joined a fortnight later by three other members of their bicycle trip, including Chrystal. Garden and Sartin were captured by the Japanese on the highway and survived the war. Two of the other cyclists were captured, escaped, and were executed when they were recaptured.

The guerrillas gave Chapman and Haywood a warm welcome when they reached their camp, including a salute from a Guard of Honour consisting of 20 young men and women. The unit numbered in all some 60 Chinese armed with a Bren gun, 3 tommy guns, 20 rifles, 5 shotguns, and 5 pistols. Some of the weapons had been recovered from the Slim River and were not in a good condition.

Shortly after they joined the guerrillas, a more senior communist called Tan Chen King arrived at the camp from Selangor. After working in the Ford factory where he had joined the Communist Party, Tan Chen King had been the interpreter at the first course held at the training school in Singapore. Chapman had taught the recruits how to identify newcomers, showing them a scar on his left knee. He was amused when Tan lifted his trouser leg to inspect the scar. Tan reported that his band of guerrillas had been working with John Davis on plans to tie up with forces in Sumatra. After crossing the Straits, Davis had returned to Malaya, gone back again to Sumatra, and then failed to make a second rendezvous again with the guerrillas in Malaya. Without his help, they were short of arms and a trained instructor. They were therefore delighted to have Chapman among them.

Maurice Cotterill, Vincent and Nona Baker, and Spencer Chapman were then in the safe hands of the guerrillas, although at risk through the shortage of food and medicine, apart from sporadic attacks by the police or the army. While they struggled to survive, the tide of Japanese conquest stemmed and then receded, turning Malaya and Singapore from an imperial asset into a military liability.

7

War Lost and Won

Hirohito was intelligent as a man, albeit fallible as a god. He had hoped in the summer and autumn of 1940 that the German air assault on Britain would be followed by a successful invasion, in which case taking possession of Malaya would present no more difficulty to him than occupying French Indochina or the Dutch East Indies. When Hitler attacked Russia on 22 June 1941 without having first defeated Britain, the Emperor ordered the Naval General Staff to make a study outlining the probable course of events after attacking Britain and the United States. The report told him that, for six months, the Japanese would be able to make great territorial gains against weak opposition. For a year after that, they would have the resources to continue fighting. Thereafter the country would become progressively weaker and would eventually lose the war. Not liking what he was told, Hirohito ordered a second study to be made independently, and was again told that Japan would only be able to prosecute the planned war successfully from October 1941 to June 1943. By then it would either have to agree peace terms or be forced to negotiate them from a constantly weakening position.

To prosecute a war of aggression successfully across the vast expanse of the Pacific Ocean, and take full advantage of the six months' grace, required control of the sea and command of the air. As the British Admiral Tom Phillips had been aware and tragically demonstrated, naval vessels other than submarines could not operate without air cover and it was not just coincidence that the 'unsinkable' German battleship, the *Bismarck*, was sunk on 27 May 1941 after an airborne torpedo had damaged its steering gear so that it would only move in circles, and that the *Prince of Wales* was destroyed after being crippled in the same way. To maintain air superiority a fleet needed aircraft carriers and for the safety of its carriers, it needed to destroy the enemy's capital ships before they came within firing range.

The Japanese had noted attentively the attack made by the British Fleet Air Arm on 11 November 1940 when 21 torpedo bombers sank three Italian battleships lying at anchor in Taranto and, in a single raid, changed the naval balance of power in the Mediterranean. If the British could do that in the mainland of Italy, a country at which they were at war, how much more might 360 planes achieve in a surprise attack on the American fleet in the Philippines before war had been declared.

Admiral Kimmel, the American commander at Pearl Harbor, had learned no lessons from Taranto. In the months leading up to December 1941 there had been a number of false alarms. Crews had been sent to action stations and then stood down without any sign of an attack. American admirals rated the Japanese carrier force as inferior to its own, including the quality of its leadership, its planes, its weapons, and its pilots. It seemed safe enough, as well as convenient, to park up eight battleships neatly at the dockside in Hawaii and to leave 600 of the 780 anti-aircraft guns on the ships unmanned as the crews spent Saturday and Sunday ashore.

The army on Hawaii was even less prepared over the

weekend, leaving only four out of 31 anti-aircraft batteries operational and, for safety, returning shells for storage away from the guns. As for the air force, its planes at Clark Field 50 miles north of Manila were neatly parked wing-tip to wing-tip to make life difficult for a saboteur but easy for the Japanese bombers, which destroyed 188 aircraft in a few hours. The loss of seven capital ships was damaging to the Americans but not fatal as, by good fortune rather than foresight, none of their three aircraft carriers had been in port.

Until two American carriers moved from the Atlantic to the Pacific, bringing the complement to five, the ten Japanese carriers ruled the seas. Their planes bombed Darwin and had the citizens of Western Australia digging slit trenches for fear of an attack. They attacked naval bases in Ceylon (today's Sri Lanka), sending the remaining British capital ships fleeing to Bombay and East Africa for safety. They protected the transports as the army occupied island after island through the Pacific, and then provided air support for operations on land. The planes they flew, whether bombers or fighters, were superior to any sea-borne aircraft operated by the British or the Americans, and their 500 pilots were of the highest quality, not merely in their ability to relocate their mother ship after a distant attack or search in the vast expanses of ocean but in the accuracy of their bombing and the techniques employed for the hazardous take-off and landing at sea.

If the Japanese showed that they could bomb an Australian city from a carrier, then the Americans could do the same to Tokyo, provided they were able to approach near enough to launch the bombers. On 18 April 1942 sixteen B-25 aircraft under the command of Colonel James Doolittle were taken on the carrier *Hornet*, accompanied by another carrier, the *Enterprise*, through the opening in the Japanese defence ring provided by Midway Island to within 650 miles of Japan and, having dropped their bombs, overflew into Chinese territory held by Chiang Kai-shek. Of the 80 aircrew, three were later executed but 71 returned safely to the United States. The significance of the raid went far beyond the trifling amount of material damage inflicted. If a hostile bomber were able to reach Tokyo, there was a risk to the sacred person of the Emperor. To prevent further raids, the Midway gap had to be closed.

From the start of hostilities, Hirohito had urged his troops to continue their thrust south. By May 1942 they had already landed on the northern side of New Guinea. It was not practicable to try to cross the island through the precipitous jungle, and the Japanese Admiral Inouye assembled a task force of three carriers to protect the troopships and other vessels as they moved on Port Moresby on the south of the island, from where Australia would be directly threatened. He knew that there were only five American carriers in the Pacific, of which *Hornet* and *Enterprise* must still be far away as a result of the Doolittle raid. On 7 May, his pilots sank a flat-topped vessel, the oiler *Neosho*, which they took to be a carrier, and reported accordingly. That left the Americans with two carriers, so he thought, against his three.

The American Admiral Chester Nimitz knew through his cryptographers of the Japanese plans. In a confused series of engagements, in which the opposing fleets missed each other sailing in opposite directions, the Americans were bombed unsuccessfully by their own land-based planes, Japanese aircraft mistakenly tried to land on American decks, and all sorts of mischances and mishaps occurred, each side lost a carrier and each had another badly damaged. What became known as the Battle of the Coral Sea led to the abandonment of the attack on Port Moresby and lifted the direct threat to Australia and New Zealand. It also proved that the Americans were now a match at sea for the hitherto invincible Japanese.

Following the Coral Sea battle, the crippled Japanese carrier *Shokaku* sailed back to Japan for major repairs. The damaged American carrier, *Yorktown*, needing a refit which would normally have taken months, returned to Hawaii on 27 May after sailing under her own steam with escorting destroyers at 10 knots. By superhuman efforts on the part of American repair teams, she was made serviceable in three days and left to join *Enterprise* and *Hornet* which had sailed for Midway two days earlier. As for the two ships that were sunk, the American crewmen on *Lexington*, and especially the pilots, were rescued to fight again, while those on *Shoho* perished.

So it was, that five months after the attacks on Malaya and Pearl Harbor, the advance to the south was stopped, a month earlier than Hirohito's studies had forecast. The most important battle of the Pacific war had still to be fought. Its outcome would determine whether the Japanese would be able to cross the ocean and make peace on favourable terms by threatening the United States mainland, or be forced back to their home islands with inevitable defeat brought closer.

On the day *Yorktown* reached Hawaii, Admiral Yamamoto sailed from Japan in his 64,000-ton flagship *Yamato* for the crucial engagement with the Americans. Under his command was a fleet of 182 vessels, including 10 battleships, 8 aircraft carriers, 24 cruisers, 70 destroyers, 15 submarines, and other auxiliary vessels. To oppose him Admiral Nimitz had 3 aircraft carriers, 8 cruisers, 14 destroyers, and 25 submarines. Yamamoto believed wrongly that the Americans had only two operational carriers, being told that *Saratoga* was on the West Coast being repaired and *Yorktown* on the seabed. In all the Japanese fleet carried 685 aircraft, along with the cream of its experienced pilots.

After leaving the Inland Sea, Yamamoto sent part of his fleet to cover an attack on the Aleutian Islands, hoping to draw the American ships away to the north. Naval intelligence in Washington thought the main thrust was aimed at Hawaii, to be followed possibly by an assault on the west coast of the United States and an attack on the Panama Canal. Fortunately Nimitz knew better.

American cryptographers, aided by the British, had broken the Japanese Navy code JN-25. They knew that Yamamoto's principal attack was to be launched against a target code-named 'AF'. The cryptographer Commander Joseph Rochefort based in Hawaii, speaking on a secure submarine cable, asked the Midway base commander to send Pearl Harbor a message stating that, because its water filtration plant was not working, they were short of fresh water, and that they should use a code which he knew had been broken by the Japanese. A few days later, a Japanese signal, read by the Americans, warned that there was a shortage of water at 'AF'. When Yamamoto's planes arrived to bomb Dutch Harbor in the Aleutians, they were amazed to find no aircraft there. Every available American plane and carrier was concentrated at Midway to await the arrival of the force under Admiral Nagumo, who was in command of the assault.

If Waterloo was a 'close-run thing', the Battle of Midway on 4 June 1942 was even closer. Successive waves of American aircraft attacked the Japanese carriers without causing any damage. At the height of the battle, the Americans had lost 44 planes, with a further 80 or more driven away, while the Japanese had lost none and no carrier had been hit by bomb or torpedo. The severity and frequency of the attacks over three hours, by planes coming at different heights from various directions, meant that Nagumo's fighters had become scattered both in terms of altitude and location. As they returned from combat, they had to refuel and take on fresh ordnance. He also had bombers and torpedo planes which needed fuelling and arming prior to take-off for attacks on the Americans.

It is not the fact, as is sometimes said, that Nagumo at 10.22 a.m. thought that the battle was already won and was preparing his bombers and torpedo planes with fuel and weapons after sending his fighters below deck, or that no Japanese fighters remained in the air at sufficient altitude to meet the last of the American dive-bombers. What is certain, however, is that the decks of all his carriers, and the aircraft hangars, were cluttered with explosives and fuel lines, while the defending airborne *Zeros* were no longer well positioned to fight off yet another attack even if it came from one direction, let alone two by dive-bombers arriving from opposite points of the compass.

The last available American aircraft from *Enterprise* were 32 dive-bombers which had failed to find the Japanese ships and landed to refuel on Midway. Searching for the Japanese carriers, they found the right bearing by taking a heading from a Japanese destroyer. When, at 10.22 a.m. on 4 June 1942, they arrived over the Japanese fleet, from the opposite direction appeared 17 dive bombers from *Yorktown*. In six minutes, three of the Japanese carriers were turned into blazing infernos. The fourth *Hiryu*, survived, only to be sunk on 9 June, having first had the consolation of seeing its pilots finally sink the *Yorktown*.

Without air cover, Yamamoto was obliged to abort his mission and return to Japan. In the space of six minutes, his fleet had lost its superiority in carriers and so command of the sea. The losses were not just of carriers and aircraft. Half her superb naval pilots had perished, as had those on *Shoho* in the Coral Sea, never to be replaced. Hirohito's close adviser, Lord Privy Seal Marquis Kido Koiichi, was told of the disaster on 6 June. He knew then that, with only two fleet carriers left, the war was lost. He gave Hirohito the news the following day.

Having made its analysis before the war that Japan would at some stage have to negotiate peace rather than win an outright victory over the United States, the Naval Staff had established a mission in Geneva so that it would have the facilities in place to reach an accommodation with the Americans on neutral territory when the right moment arrived. Finally accepting the significance of Midway, in October 1942 Hirohito sent General Okamoto Kiyotni to join the mission in Switzerland. Okamoto was a friend of the Emperor's brother, Prince Chichibu, and sending such a senior and favoured emissary was meant to show that Tokyo was sincere in wanting to negotiate peace. Okamoto was soon left in no doubt that the only deal in which the Americans, and their allies, were interested, was unconditional surrender.

Joseph Rochefort was not the only individual in the Far East to exert an influence on the course of the war much more significant than his rank or status might suggest. The Soviet spy, Richard Sorge, had long been used by the Japanese as an informal contact between themselves and their German allies. As an intermediary he was given confidential information both by the German Embassy and by sources close to the Emperor, including Marquis Kido himself, all of which he passed on to Moscow. He had, for example, been shown the secret protocols of the Tripartite Pact, under which Japan had no obligation to join Germany in an attack on Russia. In the summer of 1941 he reported that the Japanese troop movements in Manchuria were part of the 'strike south' decision taken by Hirohito, not a prelude to an attack on Soviet territory. With this information, Stalin had no need to reinforce his Asian troops: on the contrary, he could afford to weaken the frontier garrisons to make good the losses suffered in Europe in 1941.

Despite the momentous contributions each made to the Allied cause, Rochefort and Sorge met widely different fates. Rochefort, who died in 1976, was a decade later posthumously awarded the Presidential Medal of Freedom. Sorge was hanged as a spy by the Japanese on 7 November 1944.

The high tide of Japanese success had broken on the shores of New Guinea and the waters had started to recede after Midway. In five months, in addition to their successes against the British, they had achieved the conquest of the Dutch East Indies with small losses, their troops being initially greeted by many as liberators from colonialism, although the welcome might have been less enthusiastic if those liberated from the Dutch had known that Hirohito intended to retain what is now Indonesia as a Japanese colony rather than grant it independence. The Philippines, which in 1934 had been granted provisional independence from the United States, was not militarily strong enough to defend itself. Despite making many of the mistakes the British had made in Malaya, MacArthur's inexperienced troops gave the unwelcome invaders a hard fight until the island of Corregidor finally surrendered on 6 May.

Burma was defended in December 1941 by a Burmese Division, some Chinese troops, and the 17th Indian Division. The locally enlisted force, with the exception of those from the minority hill tribes, deserted rather than fight the Japanese. The Chinese quickly retreated back to China. During the retreat to Rangoon, the British contrived to blow up the only bridge across the Salween River with over half the fighting strength of the 17th Indian on the wrong side of the river. To oppose this motley enemy, General Shojira Iida had at his disposal two Divisions, in addition to which he enjoyed complete air superiority. As General Alexander retreated, Shojira was reinforced by two more Divisions and his army was only halted on the borders of India by the arrival of the monsoon.

In the battles around the Assam frontier towns on Kohima and Imphal between March and June 1944, the surrounded British/Indian troops, supplied and reinforced by air, did not surrender. With the sieges broken, the Japanese, short of food and ammunition, lost 65,000 men in their long retreat, their attrition rate being up to one hundred times greater than that of the pursuing British/Indian Divisions under General Slim.

The 1st Division of the Indian National Army, raised by the Japanese mainly from the 45,000 soldiers who surrendered in Malaya and Singapore, and the only Indian National Army (INA) unit actively to oppose the British, ceased to exist, its soldiers taking the first opportunity to surrender to their compatriots. Having retaken Burma in August 1945, General Slim was able to embark his victorious 14th Army formations at Rangoon and Madras for the British return to Malaya.

This brief summary of the global war has to be confined to events directly affecting the people who were living in Malaya— those under Japanese rule, the guerrillas of the MPAJA and British Force 136, and the handful of Europeans surviving in the jungle, such as Maurice Cotterill and Nona Baker. They heard of the fantastic claims made on the Japanese radio and in the press, and eventually of more accurate reports from the British Broadcasting Corporation (BBC). While they waited, the British victory at El Alamein in November 1942 safeguarded the oilfields of the Middle East and eliminated the threat to the Suez Canal. In February, 1943, the last German soldiers in Stalingrad, the furthest point of German advance into Russia, surrendered. In July 1943, Zhukov's victory in the Battle of Kursk proved as significant to the struggle between the Wehrmacht and the Red Army as had been Nimitz's triumph at Midway. In September 1943, Italy surrendered unconditionally. On 6 June 1944, British, American, and Canadian troops landed successfully in Normandy to drive the Germans out of France. In the Pacific American troops moved from island to island as they closed in on the Japanese mainland.

Between 2 February and 27 March 1945, Ecuador,

Paraguay, Peru, Chile, Venezuela, Turkey, Uruguay, Egypt, Syria, Lebanon, Saudi Arabia, Finland, and Argentina declared war on Germany, a trifle late, we may think, to have contributed greatly to her unconditional surrender, which took place on 8 June 1945.

8

The Japanese Occupation

While the Europeans were being herded into prison in February 1942 or, in the case of a few enterprising individuals, seeking to escape, the other races looked on with mixed emotions. The Australian gunner Russell Braddon recalled being marched through Kuala Lumpur after he had been captured, seeing severed Chinese heads on stakes at every intersection and with the crowds which had cheered them two weeks earlier now throwing stones and spitting at them as they shambled past. He was fortunate to be alive: the Malay Volunteers captured with him had been bayonetted on the spot. The victors showed more compassion to the *mems* and their children as they were being marched from the city of Singapore to their incarceration, dispersing the crowds which hurled abuse and stones at them as they passed by. A certain amount of *Schadenfreude* is understandable and these unfortunate incidents were to be compensated by the help given to prisoners in the dark years ahead by many courageous Malay and Chinese men and women at great peril to themselves.

As we noted, the Malayan economy had become integrated with those of its trading partners. The vast majority of its exports were of rubber and tin, which provided a comfortable surplus on the balance of trade. With its land less suited for the production of rice, this basic food had to be imported from its neighbours, with Burma a major supplier. From around 600,000 tons a year before the war, imports fell by 1944 to less than 100,000 tons. The peninsula also relied almost entirely on imports for oil-based products, textiles, sugar, medicines, and most manufactured goods.

From the start of the occupation, significant foreign trade came to a standstill. The United States and other industrialised countries had been the major customers for tin and rubber. Now only Japan remained, and the stocks of latex in Malaya in 1942 would have been enough to meet Tokyo's needs for the rest of the war. Apart from the 5,000 tons sent to Germany in submarines, no rubber was exported except to Japan. During the four years of the occupation 168,000 tons were produced, or a third of the total for the 12 months of 1940. Much of the wartime output was of poor quality because there was no acetic or other suitable acid available to treat the latex. Tin fared better, with production achieving a third of prewar levels by 1943 despite the fact that the deep mine at Sungei Lembing remained closed. To compound the problems, before long allied control of the seas stifled maritime trade in the Bay of Bengal as well as that between Singapore and Japan.

An immediate result of the occupation was the loss of employment by all those who had been working on any estate or mine operated under British management. We saw how Maurice Cotterill and Vincent Baker had been at pains to pay their employees before the invaders arrived. These men and women in their thousands then found themselves without any livelihood. Those employed on other rubber estates or in Chinese-owned mining operations were little better off, because there was no longer a market for their produce and, when the Japanese established controlled prices to stimulate production, they were set at such a level as to make it a waste of effort.

Elsewhere in the economy, in offices, shops, and on the land, people went back to work. In the public sector, things returned almost to normal although the Japanese stopped paying pensions to former government employees and reduced the salaries of all others. Local police officials were 're-educated' at a training centre in Singapore, the term having no sinister overtones other than impressing them with the need to serve their new masters if they wished to stay alive. Non-Japanese police were no longer allowed to carry firearms other than looted sporting guns, for which, as we will see later, an enthusiastic Malay policeman had manufactured his own cartridges – his shot embedded a half-inch steel nut in Spencer Chapman's leg. Sikhs also seemed to take readily to working for their new masters as policemen or warders although others, and especially the Chinese, were less enthusiastic. As the occupation continued and support for the new order diminished, the Japanese Police Affairs Department found it necessary to put its own nationals in charge of the larger police stations. The *Kempeitai* were ever present and handled any cases of suspected subversion or anti-Japanese behaviour. They relied heavily on torture and on informers whom they rewarded liberally.

The authorities introduced food rationing in March 1942. At first the same scale was applicable to all races but, as the quantities of food available fell, those who were Japanese, manual workers, and government employees received preferential treatment. As happened everywhere in the world at war when rationing and price controls were introduced, a black market soon developed, often unchecked in the peninsula because of the involvement of government employees and of the Japanese themselves. If rice was officially unobtainable, the public could buy on ration the filling but less nourishing tapioca, on its own or in various forms such as tapioca flour or noodles. The rice was always there on the black market for those with the means to pay.

It was inevitable that public health would suffer through malnutrition. Children born or growing up during the occupation developed physically at half the rate of their predecessors. Infant mortality increased and, among adults, the death rate doubled, especially in the cities. The shortage of medicine caused a rapid increase in the incidence of malaria, dysentery, and ulceration among the entire population, just as these conditions were to plague the refugees in the jungle. Beri-beri also became a problem due to the shortage of vitamin B in the restricted diet. In the absence of vitamin tablets or suitable food, it was treated with a variety of makeshift concoctions. Because of the unavailability of fertilisers, small-holders increased the use on their crops of untreated human sewage, which spread dysentery and cholera. The Institute for Medical research in Kuala Lumpur managed to produce vaccines against smallpox, typhoid A and B, and cholera. More often than not, these vaccines were ineffective, and in some cases they were administered only to those who prepared food. Like every other scarce commodity, vaccines became available on the black market at prices far beyond most of the population.

The cessation of imports of chemicals affected the treatment of potable water, which again increased disease. With the shortage of motor fuel, garbage remained uncollected, leading to a proliferation of flies and rats and causing yet more ill-health among the human population. Inadequacy in public health administration led to an increase in stagnant water in the towns, in which the anopheles mosquito bred. Malaria, once rare in towns and cities, became once more an urban menace and by March 1943 a member of the public needed a doctor's certificate to buy quinine. Supplies diminished as the incidence of malaria increased and there was eventually a black market in quinine sulphate which meant that only the wealthy or the Japanese enjoyed protection from the disease. Later in the occupation, the supply of quinine became subject to even stricter controls in Perak and Selangor, where the Japanese attempted to deny medication to the guerrillas.

The British had brought to the peninsula freedom under the law for the individual and, that bastion of any prosperous economy, the right to retain personal property. The Japanese made no attempt to modify the colonial justice system, although they suggested that those who now sat in judgment should use their discretion as to innocence or guilt rather than stick to the evidence before the court. As we noted earlier, the *Kempeitai* were a law unto themselves and not subject to any civil or military discipline. The army had not forgotten the lessons of Nanking and every Japanese soldier possessed the right to assault or even to kill a civilian. Few excesses led to disciplinary proceedings, as had the hospital massacre in Singapore. Even cultured Japanese officers with pro-western tendencies accepted the brutality which any private soldier might choose to display.

Malaya had before the war enjoyed a sophisticated banking system appropriate to its industrial strength. There were no less than 12 local Chinese banks, some of which were substantial concerns, while the Indian business community was served especially by the Oriental Bank of Malaya. The Japanese in Singapore had their own bank, the Yokohama Specie Bank, of which the manager was called Mutoh. Like other Japanese civilians who were not active spies, Mutoh left the city in November 1941, to reappear with the army within days of its fall. Three British institutions, the Hong Kong and Shanghai Bank, the Mercantile Bank, and the Chartered Bank were liquidated by the Japanese under Mutoh's guidance, along with American, Dutch, and French banks. Those who owed them money had the loans called in at par while depositors received only a fraction of their funds above $100—an injustice which the British banks at least were to rectify after the war.

While the Yokohama Specie Bank under Mutoh took over liquidated banks, others were allowed to continue operations, with the Chinese especially coming under strict supervision. On 11 February 1942 the British Colonial Treasurer had ordered the banks in Singapore to destroy their stocks of notes and the manager of the Hong Kong and Shanghai Bank was delighted to be able to tell Mutoh when he called to take over that the vaults held only two or three thousand dollars. The two men had, as colleagues, been on friendly terms and Mutoh did at least honour his promise to preserve documents so that the Hong Kong and Shanghai Bank could restart its business without insuperable difficulty after the war.

Prosperity needs a stable currency as well as a strong banking system. We have noted how the Japanese army and then the civil authorities issued notes which were to be on a par with the Straits dollar, and the reaction of the population to this unbacked currency. There is always an element of fiscal drag when economic circumstances change, and it was not until the summer of 1942 that people began to see the effect of shortages in terms of uncomfortable increases in the cost of living. Before the war ended, prices for freely available, locally produced articles such as fruit had increased by a factor of ten while scarcer commodities such as sugar or meat were a hundred or more times dearer. The authorities tried on occasion to curb inflation through forced loans and other financial chicanery but could not prevent the weighted cost of living rising from under 200 before the war to almost 11,000 in May 1945. Under such conditions, barter replaces currency, savings are held in gold or jewellery, and investment becomes futile. Hungry law-abiding citizens became thieves and honest administrators became corrupt.

The Japanese military administration followed closely the prewar geographical and organisational arrangements. Local government and finance was managed by a General Affairs Bureau, perhaps the single significant change to be introduced by the Japanese. In effect, the entire peninsula was being treated for the first time as a unitary state, with imperial governors in charge of each province, apart from Kedah, Perlis, Kelantan, and Trengganu which were returned to Thailand in August 1943 as a reward for Thai help prior to the invasion. This experience of running the country as a single Japanese colony proved a significant factor in the creation of conditions on which the modern state of Malaysia could be based.

Initially the conquerors decided that the Sultans had no part to play in the new order, Hirohito being the sole benevolent and absolute ruler. Threatened with the loss of their titles, authority, and wealth, in April 1942 the Sultans saw Yamashita in Singapore to congratulate him on his brilliant victory and to pledge their support for the Japanese. By the end of the year, Tokyo realised that it had made a mistake in ignoring or alienating these popular rulers and when he visited Malaya in July 1943, Tojo went out of his way to thank the Sultans for their help during the invasion and thereafter. In October 1943 they were appointed Vice-President of the State Advisory Councils and from then until the return of the British they retained their status.

The Japanese varied their approach to relationships with the Malays, the Chinese, and the Indians. Before the occupation there had not been a serious Malay independence movement or widespread resentment against colonial rule such as existed in Burma or the Dutch East Indies. The Kesatuan Malaya Muda (KMM), a Malay party seeking independence, had been in touch with the Japanese before the invasion and its leaders may have expected great things when the British were driven out. As we have seen, the conqueror was uninterested in any constitutional arrangement for Malaya other than establishing another colony such as Korea or Formosa, and the KMM was banned in June 1942. With the former British administrators in prison, their deputies, usually Malays in the Malay Administrative Service, were promoted in their place, although always responsible ultimately to a Japanese official. Along with other races, Malays also served on the State Advisory Councils. This experience in rule and administration, without the discredited British in charge, not only demonstrated that they could govern themselves: it also gave them a taste for self-government.

Estimates of the number of Chinese massacred by the occupiers in 1942 in their campaign of screening and terror go as high as 100,000. Whether members of the Communist Party, the *Kuomintang*, or non-political, every Chinese person had good reason to oppose Japanese rule. They remembered the Rape of Nanking and it is possible that they also received news of the massacres ordered by Hirohito on 20 April 1942 as a result of which Japanese troops under General Okamura Yasuji inflicted collective punishment on Chunking province because its villagers had helped some of Doolittle's aircrew to escape. In their rampage they killed around 250,000 people, of whom the majority were civilians. With almost exactly 100,000 more Chinese people than Malays living in Malaya and Singapore in 1941, the Japanese soon learned that they had to placate this numerous and industrious group if they wished to run the country. The Chinese community was not a single bloc but fragmented, not just between immigrants and those who had been born locally but also between the different ethnic groups and languages.

It is not surprising that the Indian community was the most sympathetic to the occupier. The Indian Independence League (IIL) under its Secretary-General, Pritam Singh, was in touch with the Japanese before the war. Talks between Pritam Singh, the Japanese, and Mohan Singh held in Taiping on 31 December 1941 led to the foundation of the Indian National Army or Japanese Indian Freedom Fighters (JIFFs). Mohan Singh was a Captain in the British/Indian army and became Commanding Officer of the INA. He was to claim that 42,000 Indian prisoners of war joined the INA, while 13,000 chose imprisonment. Wavell put the number of turncoats at only 20,000, but that is too low. Because the INA was dominated by Sikhs, it was less popular with Tamils, although many unemployed tappers enlisted simply to have something for themselves and their families to eat. Both the IIL and the INA remained ineffective until Subhas Chandra Bose, the former President of the Congress party and Lord Mayor of Calcutta, took over the Presidency of the IIL on 4 July 1943. On 21 October he formed a Provisional Government of Free India with himself as Head of State as well as assuming other senior offices and on 24 October his government declared war on Britain and the United States. His gesture went unnoticed by his enemies and his soldiers declined to fight against their fellow-countrymen of the 14th Army when they met them. Meanwhile, for the 750,000 Indians living in Malaya, and the rest of the population, life became hard and, while their enthusiasm for Indian independence did not diminish, their trust in the Japanese did.

We will examine later the struggle to grow food, which had lasting effects on the country and the economy, including deforestation, the cessation of rubber-tapping, the invasion of Malay reservations, and the squatter phenomenon. Unemployment was replaced by a shortage of labour as the conqueror conscripted men to work on public and defence works in Malaya and on the Burma railway. As to the morality of collaboration with the conqueror, we should reflect that in Holland, until the tide of war turned in 1944, only 1 per cent of the population had been active in the resistance, while the figure for France was even lower. Terror and the need to eat are strong deterrents to opposition to a ruthless occupying power. What is remarkable about Malaya and Singapore under the Japanese is not that there were so few who resisted the new imperialism, but that there were so many.

9

Living with the Guerrillas

In the eyes of the MPAJA, all non-communist armed bands living in the jungle and opposing the Japanese were bandits. In Johore especially, some of the guerrillas were not Chinese and others were Chinese Nationalists rather than communists, adherents of Chiang Kai-shek rather than Mao or Stalin. The group Maurice Cotterill joined near Palong in Negri Sembilan seems to have had no political affiliation. Chapman described them as 'cheerful and likeable rogues' although 'first-class guerrilla material and thirsting to have a crack at the Jap'. Before the occupation the nucleus of the band had been unlicensed distillers of *samsu*, a sprit which they sold illegally in Segamat. When the war brought that business to an end, they collected whatever arms they could find and lived by robbing *towkays*, such as Leong Kee and Ah Fong, leaving them always sufficient assets for the continuation of their businesses.

For a while Maurice and Brian Tyson enjoyed a more comfortable lifestyle with their band than the MPAJA allowed in its camps. The leader of the group lived in a hut, with the luxury of a corrugated iron roof, sharing the accommodation with his female companion and the two Europeans. Many of the other men also lived with women, some of them Malays whom they had abducted. As might be expected from their prewar occupation, *samsu* was freely available nor was the band forbidden opium. As a result of their raids, they were not short of money and their diet included many luxuries such as tinned food. The two Europeans supplemented the meat supply by shooting pig and monkey, with Tyson spending most of his time out hunting, although he remained far from fit.

The gang was comparatively well armed, despite having thrown away boxes of grenades because they didn't know what they were. The numbers Maurice and Spencer Chapman mentioned for the quantity of their weapons differed widely. For example, Chapman says that they had two machine guns, which Maurice does not mention. Both agree, however, that they had two tommy guns and more than 20 rifles, as well as the two pistols contributed by the Europeans. They also had abundant ammunition. Aware of the plenitude of weaponry, the MPAJA were anxious to absorb the group, ideological issues apart. For what turned out to be excellent reasons, Maurice distrusted the communists and opposed any surrender of the band's independence.

In the summer of 1942 the Japanese authorities sought to eliminate the guerrillas operating from the jungle fringes by cutting off their food supply. Japanese and Malay police raided villages which they suspected of supplying food, killing the inhabitants and burning the houses but leaving other buildings such as the mosque unharmed. In the case of the Palong gang, some of the villagers fled to the jungle. Guerrillas with rifles at once set off to confront the police, arriving too late to catch them. Following the attack, the village site and the formerly cultivated land around it remained deserted, whereupon the gang and the surviving villagers moved in, finding plenty of pig, which came to eat the tapioca and the rubber nuts. There was also an abundance of bananas, papaya, grapefruit, *cempedak*, and jackfruit. Compared with the strict regime, shortage of food, and discomfort of the MPAJA camps, it was a paradise. When Chapman stayed there for a week, he said it reminded him of a Scottish glen.

In their attempts to induce the Palong gang to join forces with them, the MPAJA patrol from Triang, which was about 30 miles away in Pahang, had sent as emissaries two young bespectacled Marxist fanatics whose credibility and persuasive powers were diminished by their insistence that their prospective converts should learn Mandarin and sing *The Red Flag*. After a few days of ridicule, and fearing for their lives, the missionaries slipped out of the camp at night and rejoined their patrol. The MPAJA then decided to use Chapman as their go-between and in August 1942 allowed him to send a letter to Maurice suggesting that they should meet. This contact with a fellow-European would not have been sanctioned by the communists, nor would the letters have been delivered, without some ulterior motive. Negotiations by letter continued inconclusively for some months. When these failed, the MPAJA arranged to send Chapman with an English-speaking companion, Ah Ching, to see if a meeting face-to-face would persuade Maurice to put pressure on his comrades to join forces with them.

The men met in January 1943. Chapman says it happened on New Year's Day, while Maurice Cotterill says it was not until 18 January 1943. Tyson was by then a very sick man, probably suffering from pneumonia. Socially, the meeting was a success and, for Chapman, a rare chance to chat to a fellow-countryman in English. Tyson and Maurice had previously instructed the gang in the use of their weapons but, as Chapman saw it, to little effect, and he gave them a series of lectures in the deserted mosque. As Ah Ching could not speak the gang's dialect and they could not speak Mandarin, the lectures had to be given in Malay, with Maurice translating the difficult bits. Chapman wrote later that these were the best pupils he ever had and that his days there were the happiest he spent in the jungle. It had been a long time since he had seen a European and he was disappointed when Maurice refused to return with him or to put pressure on the gang to join the MPAJA.

Chapman found the shooting around the deserted village excellent and bagged a pig every day. On one occasion when he was out with his gun, he saw coming towards him members of the gang, wearing their Australian bush hats, having been to a kampong to buy rice. He unwisely left cover to join them and was greeted with a hail of bullets. Fortunately he had proved no more effective at weapon training than the two men he disparaged, and he escaped unscathed. He reached the camp before his attackers and was interested to hear them boast, on their return, of having annihilated a large force of Japanese.

So long as the Palong guerrillas refused to join the communists, Maurice used Tyson's weakness as an excuse for staying with them. Failing in their mission, Chapman entrusted his diaries to Maurice for safe keeping and departed with Ah Ching on 26 January 1943 to rejoin the MPAJA. At five o'clock that afternoon Brian Tyson died and he was buried an hour later. Maurice sent a runner to apprise Chapman of the death, and Chapman returned to see if Maurice was all right and to persuade him to leave, now that Tyson was dead. In *The Jungle is Neutral*, Chapman writes that he was still at the camp when Tyson died, but his recollection is incorrect. With Tyson's illness no longer a pretext for staying, Maurice excused himself by saying that he had developed a fever and was not up to making a move, although he might do so later.

In the next few weeks the MPAJA from Triang failed to deliver letters between the two Europeans, fearful, so Maurice thought, that Chapman might leave them and throw in his lot with the Palong gang. In June 1943 another MPAJA regiment from the Segamat area told them that they must stop their robbery, in return for which the communists would supply them with food. Faced with an ultimatum, they had to agree and that four of the MPAJA should remain with them. From now on, they lost not just their independence but their access to a healthy diet, or sometimes to any food at all.

In the summer of 1943 the Sikh police chief in Jelebu vowed to destroy the guerrillas in his area. As the tracks leading to the camps were booby-trapped, Japanese troops made the police or soldiers from the INA lead the assaults. This had for them the advantage that the initial casualties were Indians or Malays but it diminished the chances of achieving surprise. The gang at Palong was about 70 strong that summer when it was attacked by around 100 police and Japanese. Although most of the riflemen were away from the camp, they stood and fought, killing nine of the attackers with only two of their men being injured. To avoid the inevitable follow-up, they moved further into the jungle where they were again attacked by a larger, better organised group, probably, in the absence of booby-traps, of Japanese soldiers rather than the INA or the police. This time the attackers managed to surround the camp which meant that no food could get through.

The guerrillas escaped by stealing away by night, abandoning everything they could not carry with them, and made for the Segamat area. After marching for four days with very little to eat, they found a deserted settlement with some tapioca growing. Here they were attacked again and decided to move on to Tasek in Pahang, where there was likely to be more food. The ensuing journey through the jungle took them a further six days and the group arrived at their new campsite in a weakened condition, having had almost nothing to eat on the way.

Food remained a problem in their new camp and they were reduced to eating tapioca leaves as a vegetable, usually without oil or salt. They were attacked only once more by the Japanese, of whom they killed two and wounded others, losing two of their own men. With a diet deficient in vitamin B, and general debility, Maurice went down with beri-beri and the recurrent malaria.

Spencer Chapman, with his companion Haywood, had joined No. 5 Independent Anti-Japanese Regiment at the Ulu Slim camp in April 1942. He knew that, once he had thrown in his lot with the communists, he would be their prisoner. They needed him as an instructor and also because he knew where the 'stay-behind' parties had hidden dumps of arms and ammunition. The guerrillas clearly held him in high regard, calling him 'Chippie', or their white leader. There were in all eight MPAJA regiments, of which seven included men who had been trained at the No. 101 Special Training School in Singapore. The exception was the unit operating in Pahang, with whom the Bakers had sought refuge. The regiments were to a large extent autonomous, especially after 1 September 1942 when the Party leadership was massacred at a meeting at the Batu Caves through a betrayal by its Secretary-General, Lai Tek, who was working as an agent for the Japanese.

Procedure varied from camp to camp. In the most organised, each day had the same programme of parades, military drill and training, lessons in Mandarin, foraging, housekeeping, bathing, eating, and political lectures. The strength of a regiment remained at around 100, including a few young women, with recruits being brought in for instruction and then returned to live in the kampongs. The object was always to have as many trained reserves available in the community outside as were living in the jungle. The regiments depended for much of their food, other than meat, fish, and some tapioca, on supplies from neighbouring villages, which resulted in many of them being sacked and their inhabitants murdered by the police and the Japanese. From within the jungle they shot, caught, or gathered pigs, snakes, turtles, monkeys, and fish, along with the tapioca. Nona Baker reported that on occasion she also ate young crocodiles, lizards, bear, tiger, deer, and, on a single occasion, tapir and elephant.

Informers were the greatest danger and any suspicion of treachery among the guerrillas or their supporters was dealt with ruthlessly. Those still living in the camp were shot, often on flimsy evidence, and those outside were hunted down and killed. Nona Baker related an incident which illustrates the lengths to which her companions went to protect themselves. A *towkay*, who had been visiting the camp, returned to the town without permission. Shortly afterwards a stranger was seen in the jungle nearby. On the suspicion that he might have been connected with the *towkay* and up to no good, he was brought into the camp and killed. Despite these sanctions, the problem of informers persisted right through the war. As the Chinese had the most information, they also posed the greatest threat.

Because food was always scarce, the more disciplined regiments ensured that all those who were actively working received equal rations, with stealing a capital offence. Inevitably, when supplies were very low, the senior people saw it as their duty to maintain their own strength even if the rank and file suffered. Nona Baker saw how four guerrillas who had been stealing food within the camp were tortured for a week before they were killed. A lad who proved squeamish about taking part in the slaughter was later made to kill an Indian dresser, whom we would today call a paramedic. The Indian had been found near the camp looking for herbs in the jungle and his skills were much in demand in the regiment. Despite Nona's pleas, he refused to give an undertaking not to escape and said he would not help the communists. They would not risk releasing him and so they murdered him. Life in the jungle with the communists was not for the faint-hearted.

Those in the MPAJA camps enjoyed no luxuries such as *samsu* or a pipe of opium and the songs they sang were no more catchy than *The Red Flag* or the *Internationale*. Despite the presence of young women, sex was taboo. It is not surprising that many recruits decided to quit the uncomfortable, hazardous, and monastic life in the jungle for a more normal existence outside.

The MPAJA leadership soon recognised that hit-and-run raids against the Japanese only stirred up trouble unnecessarily, both for the guerrillas and for the local inhabitants. In any case, before 1944 the regiments were not sufficiently equipped to form any serious military threat. Communism was the driving force and passion of their leaders. The regiments were anti-Japanese but not pro-British. It was left to John Davis to broker the agreement which placed 10,000 trained and armed guerrillas on the exposed flank of the Japanese supporting the British/Indian forces in August 1945.

We noted how, in March 1942, Chapman and several other British refugees, had tried to reach the coast riding bicycles on the roads at night. He and Haywood had given up the attempt short of Tanjung Malim and taken to the jungle. His two companions in the fortnight of sabotage before the fall of Singapore, who had been following them, had been captured. However difficult it might be to travel through the jungle, that experience should have been proof that no European could move on the roads even at night except on foot without risking his life and that of his companions.

Faced with travelling 50 miles to the Sungei Gow camp near Karak where they had stashed arms, Chapman and Haywood agreed to risk going by bicycle at night on minor roads which, the MPAJA assured them, were not patrolled by the police. They set off early in May 1942. On the second night, in bright moonlight, Chapman and Haywood stopped a few miles short of their destination for the Chinese to catch up. They were overtaken by three Malay policemen on bicycles, one of them with a double-barrelled shotgun over his handlebars.

Although Chapman had a loaded revolver, he gave the policeman a violent push rather than shoot him, on the grounds that his enemies were the Japanese, not the Malays. This sentiment was not reciprocated. As the Europeans pedalled furiously away, the policeman let fly with both barrels, puncturing Chapman's tyre and imbedding the half-inch nut in his leg. Hearing the gunfire as they arrived on the scene, Chapman's Chinese escort abandoned their bicycles and crawled into the jungle to join Chapman and Haywood. When the policemen followed them, Chapman dropped the man with the gun, who managed to fire another two rounds despite being hit in the arm and leg. His fellows then fled. Chapman was relieved to learn after the war that, after being admitted to Bentong hospital, the courageous policeman recovered. The incident should, however, have taught him and the MPAJA two important lessons. At that stage of the war, some at least of the Malay police were committed supporters of the Japanese: and it was not safe for Europeans to venture out of the jungle by day or night.

After this encounter both Chapman and Haywood became ill. When Chapman was again mobile they uncovered and handed over a substantial armoury of weapons and ammunition to the Pahang MPAJA. They now needed to return to Perak. Haywood was too sick to walk far and they decided to risk travelling by car at night, with armed men on the running-boards, even though the Japanese had by this time disabled, and forbidden the use of, all private cars. They left on 11 July and had not gone far when they saw the headlights of a truck coming towards them. Both vehicles stopped. While his companions made for the jungle, Chapman lobbed two grenades into the back of the lorry, killing six of the 42 Japanese soldiers and injuring others. He was hit twice, receiving minor wounds. The MPAJA driver of the car and Haywood were killed and two others were injured.

The survivors were 14 miles from Menchis and, after the slaughter, knew they had to clear the area before daylight. They met on the road a barricade which was fortunately manned by Chinese police, and were allowed to pass. After an arduous trek, Chapman reached the camp of the Menchis guerrillas on 13 July 1942 having lost all his money and everything except the clothes he wore, his revolver, his watch, and his binoculars. It is from this camp that he was sent by the MPAJA to talk to Maurice Cotterill and Brian Tyson.

Chapman had, as we noted, given his first diary to Chrystal for safekeeping, only for the Japanese to get hold of it. While he was lying wounded and still under fire from the Japanese in the lorry incident on 11 July, he buried his second diary, which was later found by the Sakai and handed to the Japanese. His third diary he entrusted to Maurice Cotterill to look after, and the Japanese captured that also. Before the war ended they were to recover two more. We will never know how much useful information the occupiers gleaned from these diaries, or whether any helper was betrayed through them. The obsession with having a record available for posterity may give a clue as to Chapman's character. He, more than anyone, should have known that the keeping of a diary is both unwise and forbidden for any soldier on active service.

The MPAJA regiment which the Bakers joined had several outposts. At each of these they cultivated ground for vegetables and built semi-permanent accommodation around a parade ground. If the living quarters were cramped, they were at least dry. The Japanese knew that Vincent was living with the guerrillas not far from Kuantan and were anxious to capture him. The MPAJA were as keen to keep him alive because they were using his status to extract levies from *towkays* in Kuantan. Lao Lee, the senior commander, decided that Vincent and Nona would be safer if they were sent to the regimental headquarters at Sungei Riau. This was a well-organised camp, with a large parade ground and a facility for printing propaganda. Orders were sent from the camp not merely to outlying detachments of the MPAJA but also to the *min yuen*, or communist sympathisers in the kampongs, who provided information and food for the guerrillas, and gave them warning of impending Japanese assaults.

All the European refugees in the jungle complained from time to time of boredom, and idleness was bad for their mental and physical fitness. Reading a page of music in the camp office one day, Nona hummed the tune. The guerrillas were amazed at this ability to read music, although it was unremarkable in one who had been a music teacher. From then on, she was given the job of choir mistress, the singing of communist songs being a feature of camp life. Vincent had no specific task and too much time on his hands for morbid reflection.

In May 1943 the MPAJA, being very short of weapons, decided to retrieve the equipment which Cotterill, Tyson, and Chiang had hidden when Davis had told them to report to Segamat in January, 1942. The other person who knew where the cache was situated was the electrician Fanseca, who was by then in charge of the Kuantan electricity-generating station. Lao Lee decided to take Nona and Vincent back to Sungei Lembing with a strong escort, arranging to meet Fanseca, who had made a map of the burial site, in a house on the outskirts of Kuantan. It was an emotional reunion for both men. Fanseca was horrified to see how gaunt and feeble the *tuan besar* had become while Vincent was touched by Fanseca's courage in providing a news service based on monitoring broadcasts from London and his confidence that the British would return. Knowing the risk Fanseca was taking, the Bakers and Lao Lee urged him to join them in the jungle. He refused, saying that it was his duty to see that, with all the Japanese propaganda, people heard the truth until the British returned.

Nona went with Lao Lee to find the hiding place. Already it was difficult to move through rubber plantations because they had not been weeded and the avenues between the trees were full of rank grass. Former miners had cut down so much of the forest on the edge of the jungle to cultivate the land for food that the topography had been changed. Having located the cache with difficulty, they found that everything of any value to them had already been stolen.

On 16 September 1943 Lao Lee announced to the regiment that he had heard through the *min yuen* that the Japanese were about to make a major thrust against their camps and intended to cut off their supply of food. For their greater security, Vincent and Nona were sent to a remote camp which was commanded by Lao Fong, an ardent communist who relished the chance of harming someone who had been the most important capitalist in the state. Lao Fong vindictively denied the Europeans adequate food or medical attention and they were both seriously ill when Lao Lee heard what was happening and visited them. He was horrified at their condition, dismissed Lao Lee, and ordered that both Vincent and Nona should have special rations to restore their health. By this time Vincent was suffering from beri-beri and malaria, and may well have also contracted pneumonia. As the Japanese attacks persisted, the Bakers were moved to an isolated hut, where, with Japanese troops on the rampage, they remained on their own for four days. By the time the guerrillas were able to visit them, Vincent was dead.

The Japanese destroyed all but one of the Pahang MPAJA camps and their associated food plantations. There were many casualties on both sides. Fortunately Lao Lee survived, to reconstruct the regiment. Nona, suffering from beri-beri and with a leg so badly infected that she could not walk, was moved to the one surviving guerrilla plantation, where she gradually regained her strength. It is there that we must leave her while we take a further look at the hardships facing everyone else living in Malaya and Singapore under Japanese rule.

10

Hardship and Cruelty

We examined earlier the conditions under which civilians lived under Japanese occupation and how the virtual cessation of the international trade on which the Malay economy depended led to increasing privation. We also noted that the initial unemployment among miners and estate workers was replaced, as the occupation continued, with a shortage of labour. The relocation of a significant proportion of the population, either through forced labour or in the drive to grow food, led to permanent changes in Malayan society. Sympathisers among the half a million people, most of them Chinese, squatting in what had been rubber estates, forest fringe, or Malay Reservations provided the food supply on which first the MPAJA and then the communist guerrillas in the Emergency depended. Now we must look at the use by the Japanese of slave labour and the effect of that policy on society at large.

In the early days of the occupation, the conquerors used prisoners of war rather than civilians as conscripted labour for tidying up war damage, improving airfields, moving stores, and various other public works. Unlike the American prisoners taken in the Philippines and Guam, those in Malaya were not usually sadistically treated, although the directives of the Prisoner of War Management Section in Tokyo indicated to local commanders that the ultimate policy was their extermination. As the Nazis acted towards the Jews, so Tokyo envisaged the long-term treatment of its non-Asiatic prisoners, extracting whatever benefit they could from their labour before they died. It was not just on the whim of the local commandant that the last task set to European prisoners in Sumatra in August 1945 was the digging of their own mass graves, which happily they did not have to fill. Contrary to many post-war reports, some officers commanding the prisoner of war camps sought to alleviate the severity of their instructions from the Imperial Staff, especially as the prospect of defeat loomed. Few of the uneducated Japanese or Korean guards showed similar humanity.

When Japan lost control of the sea at Midway, it also lost the ability to strike at Hawaii or to retain its conquests in the Pacific. Apart from the fighting in China, which had no direct impact on the Anglo-Americans, the only theatre in which Hirohito could profitably deploy his troops against them was in Burma. In this theatre he was able to threaten India and so put pressure on his opponents to agree to a negotiated settlement. The Japanese Divisions in Burma were supplied by sea through the Bay of Bengal or through poor overland routes from Thailand. It was not long before the sea route became precarious, with British and Dutch submarines sinking traffic between Singapore and Rangoon. For the army in Burma seriously to threaten India, land-based communications from Japan through China, Indochina, and Siam had to be improved as a matter of urgency.

If Napoleon's armies marched on their stomach, the emperor's marched on the railway. In 1942, the track came to an end some forty miles west of Bangkok. Between that terminus and the railhead in Burma at Thanbyuzayat lay over 200 miles of jungle and swamp, split by ridges and gullies, a land infested with mosquitoes and almost bereft of habitation. British engineers, dreaming of a railway from Singapore to Calcutta, had surveyed the route and decided that it was impracticable for a railway, although they had left a trail indicating a possible line to follow. Faced with enormous logistical problems in Burma, the Japanese High Command made the bridging of the gap between the two rail networks a matter of the highest priority, however difficult the terrain or inhospitable the climate. They were able to use for some of the metals, as we noted, the abandoned line south from Kota Bharu. For labour, they had an expendable resource in the prisoners of war and in the local population of their recently conquered territories. The first Australian prisoners, 3,000 of them, arrived at Thanbyuzayat on 1 October 1942. Another 1,500 prisoners lost their lives when the vessel carrying them from Singapore to Rangoon was torpedoed and sunk.

Ex-prisoners have written in graphic and moving detail about their experiences on the railway. It is incomprehensible that the Japanese, with the best railway engineers in the world, set about its construction, so vital to their strategic plans, in such an inefficient and inhumane manner. By the time the 250 miles or so of metals had been laid, 12,568 of the 61,000 British, Australian, American, and Dutch prisoners of war sent to build it had died. The survivors of the other 250,000 civilian conscripts sent to work on the line alongside the prisoners of war have left fewer accounts of their ordeal The soldiers had training in hygiene, a few intrepid medical staff to treat them, and their comradeship, which helped to keep them alive. The Malays and Tamils, the Burmese, Thais, and Javanese deposited in the wilderness of cholera, dysentery, beri-beri, and malaria as starved slave labour had no such advantages. We cannot know for sure how many of these wretched men died because the Japanese were not as scrupulous in counting their victims as were their German allies. The best guess is that between 77,000 and 92,000 of the workers on the railway, other than the prisoners of war, did not return home. It was little consolation that the outbreak in June 1943 of *vibrio comma*, a particularly nasty strain of cholera which stopped work on the line for a week, was as fatal to the guards as it was to their charges.

The railway opened on 25 October 1943. The 331,000 men sent to work on it had moved 150 million cubic feet of earth and left in its path a corpse for every thirteen feet of track. Most of the camps of the labourers were abandoned early in 1944 and the survivors sent back to Changi jail or allowed to return home. The Japanese kept back some of the prisoners of war and Malays to repair the collapsed sections of bridges and the embankments, some of which had been sabotaged in the original construction, and then to deal with the havoc caused by repeated air attacks. Some of the prisoners even came to resent the damage their compatriots were doing when their precious railway was bombed. For the maintenance gangs, the rations and living conditions improved. Newsreel footage of the survivors when they were freed by the 14th Army shows that they were not nearly as emaciated as those who had been returned to Singapore in 1943. Either the Japanese and Korean guards had realised that live men work better than corpses, or they were fearful of what might happen to themselves when the war ended. Today the line lies abandoned, except for the section which remains a tourist attraction.

Approximately 73,500 of the civilians who worked on the Burma railway came from Malaya and almost exactly 25,000 of them perished. This was, however, only one of many projects for which the Japanese in the peninsula required forced labour. With the railway south from Kota Bharu out of action, they constructed a highway down the eastern side of the country. In March 1943 they sent workers from Malaya to Borneo to build an airfield and to Sumatra in April 1944 to build a railway across the island. Others were used within the peninsula for the construction of military bunkers and elaborate defence systems of the sort which were to take such a toll of the American Marines on Iwo Jima. Elsewhere the conscripted workers built anything from new airfields to accommodation for displaced town-dwellers. Just as on the railway, the death rate from malaria and malnutrition remained high and even in Malacca a project involving 2,500 slave workers would see three or four men a day die.

Initially, the Japanese told recruits for these construction projects that they would be away for only a short time and would be given leave to return home every fifty days. They were promised $1 a day, with free food and lodging. In addition their dependants would be paid $15 a month or, ominously, a gratuity of $120 if they died. As the pool of unemployed people dried up and the public learned the true conditions of their employment, the daily wage on offer increased to $20 a day. There were no longer any takers. Faced with the absence of volunteers, the authorities resorted to compulsion. In December 1943 they established a Labour Service Corps which required that a percentage of any community must work on specified strategic projects. By the end of 1944, new regulations sought to bar all men of working age from doing anything which did not help the Japanese war effort. From 1 April 1945 so severe had the shortage of labour become that it became illegal for men to work in many jobs in service industries. To alleviate the shortage of manpower, as in Britain, women were encouraged to take on what had previously been a man's job.

An unfortunate consequence for the Japanese of the forced labour policy was that many young men, and particularly those among the Chinese community, went into the jungle to offer their services, or seek refuge, with the MPAJA. Nona Baker reported that in her Regiment none of these refugees was turned away, despite their lack of political commitment, and this influx contributed to the rapid increase in the strength of the guerrillas in 1944 and 1945.

The distortion of the economy by the diversion of labour to public works was paralleled by movement of the people following the drive to grow more food. Imports of rice from Burma, Thailand, and Indochina did not cease altogether but fell in 1942 to less than half the prewar total of nearly 600,000 tons and then continued to diminish as transport by sea became more hazardous. Because larger boats were being sunk, the production of shallow-draft wooden junks boomed. A single successful voyage by one of these vessels importing rice, especially if it was sold on the black market, was profitable enough to pay for the junk's construction. The demand for these vessels was such that shipwrights soon ran out of seasoned wood and vessels made out of green timber were fortunate to survive more than a single trip.

The Japanese made great efforts to encourage rice production, including the introduction of new, and potentially more productive, strains from Formosa. Paddy fields require the control of water levels which, in places, also involves irrigation. Irrigation projects had first been introduced in Perak at the end of the 19th century. Under Japanese rule, as with other public utilities, their maintenance was neglected. The systems further deteriorated because the felling of trees on sloping ground led to soil erosion. The soil washed away changed the nature of the rivers into which it was deposited and this in turn clogged up the irrigation systems which they fed. Wet rice produces twice the crop per acre of dry rice. Although the area planted with wet rice in the war years remained constant, with inadequate control of water supply productivity plummeted. The area planted with dry rice doubled, but from a comparatively low base. Other factors affecting rice production were the low price set by the Japanese and the reluctance of growers to sell their produce on the open market. For all these reasons, between 1942 and 1946, instead of the planned increase in rice production and self-sufficiency, the annual crop fell from about 335,000 to 227,000 tons.

Because of the shortage of rice, tapioca and root crops became staple foods. Nona Baker remarked on the change in the topography at Sungei Lembing brought about by the invasion of the jungle by displaced mine workers to make arable land. The same phenomenon occurred throughout the peninsula. With no ground available for vegetable cultivation in the towns, hungry people moved to places where they could grow their own crops. The policy of reserving land for the exclusive use of Malays was fundamental to British Malaya and to the compact with the Rulers. Just as the Japanese abandoned the control of the forests, so in December 1942 they opened Malay Reservations to non-Malays. Rubber tapping had virtually ceased in 1943 and the authorities directed that on each estate trees should be felled and the ground given over to food. As with many Japanese edicts, especially later in the war, compliance was at best patchy, with estate owners unwilling to destroy productive trees even if they were not being tapped at the time.

The inhabitants of Singapore were less able to supplement their rations by growing food than those living elsewhere. In 1943 the Japanese proposed moving 300,000 people from the city to settlements on the mainland or other islands. They made some preparations, using forced labour, for the reception of these displaced persons. A town dweller, however, handed a plot of land riddled with roots and on which felled tree trunks still lay and without any experience in horticulture was no better off than he and his family had been in the city. Malay villagers often helped their new neighbours with advice on everything from constructing a house to growing crops. The authorities also issued explanatory leaflets on horticulture, along with their usual propaganda exhortations. None of these aids turned town dwellers into farmers overnight.

Large areas were allocated by the Japanese for food production, and the combination of hunger and compulsion moved many of the population from an urban to a rural environment. The Malays had been the traditional farmers, although the Chinese were skilled gardeners. Now the

Chinese also had to learn farming. Half of them prior to 1941 had not been born in Malaya and many of these immigrants might have been expected to return whence they came when their working life ended. The wartime dispersal of population was an important factor in turning them from expatriates into permanent residents.

One other section of the population was forcibly relocated. Cotterill, Baker, and Chapman all report how villagers in kampongs suspected of helping the guerrillas were, in the early days, simply massacred. Later in the war, when locally recruited police needed to think of the future, they were merely evicted. No arrangements were made, as later in the Emergency, for them to subsist elsewhere, but at least the men, women, and children were no longer just murdered.

For many people illness and malnutrition followed by relocation became the salient features of Japanese Co-Prosperity. The constraints of hunger changed the nature of Malayan society. Shortages, especially of food, were to be among the problems which faced the British/Indian forces when they landed in September 1945.

11

Force 136 and the Final Years in the Jungle

The radio transmitters available to soldiers in 1942 were cumbersome machines. Short-wave receivers were smaller and more easily concealed, which meant that it was impossible for the Japanese to suppress entirely the dissemination of news from British and American sources. The hazardous task of receiving and relaying the news was undertaken by brave men such as Fanseca in Kuantan and the equally courageous teacher, P. G. Pamadsasa, who was tortured and executed in Malacca after being betrayed for concealing a short-wave radio, leaving a moving testament in which he said, 'I have always cherished British sportsmanship, justice and the Civil Service as the finest things in an imperfect world. I die for these.' The contribution of such men to the downfall of the Japanese was inestimable because they were able to demonstrate the falsity of Japanese news, giving those who had accepted the occupation second thoughts, while others were encouraged actively to resist it.

News was still getting into the country but none was getting out until, late in 1942, Lai Ping Khiong travelled from Singapore through Malaya, Thailand, and Indochina into China whence he was flown to India. Here he provided information about the Japanese military strength in the peninsula and, more importantly, about the nucleus of a guerrilla movement in the jungle, led by communists trained in Singapore by the Special Operations Executive (SOE). The SOE had established in Ceylon a unit like the No. 101 Special Training School and in

July of that year it established a Malayan Section. This drew recruits from Chinese and Malay speakers who had been out of the country when it fell, including seamen who had been in foreign ports and those who had been studying abroad. One trainee, Lim Bo Seng, who had been attending university in Hong Kong, went back Chungking to recruit volunteers from others like him who were still in Nationalist China. After training, the men, including two nephews of Tunku Abdul Rahman, were posted to a unit called Force 136.

Having learned what was happening in Malaya and Singapore under the Japanese, Force 136 needed to establish a radio transmission station there and to make contact with the guerrillas. The only aircraft with the endurance for the return flight from India was the *Catalina*, which provided a sitting target for *Zero* fighters. The Straits of Malacca are shallow and no British submarine then in service was sufficiently small to approach the mangrove-ridden shores or beaches close enough to put men ashore. Fortunately there were two Dutch submarines which met the need. The next question was who should be sent, which is where we again meet John Davis.

After opening the escape route through Sumatra in February 1942, Davis had gone back to Malaya to meet members of a 'stay-behind' party behind Japanese lines. He returned to Sumatra but was unable to keep a second rendezvous in Malaya because Singapore had fallen and Sumatra was under attack. To escape capture, he sailed in a small boat the 1,000 miles to Ceylon, a journey taking 35 days. On arrival, he was inducted into the army as an officer in the Rajputana Rifles and posted to the SOE in Ceylon. On a

Chinese language course in Hong Kong before the war he had met a fluent speaker of Chinese dialects, R. N. Broome, from the Chinese Protectorate. These two men, with Spencer Chapman, were to provide leadership to the British element of the guerrilla movement in Malaya.

Davis was sent by submarine to Kedah in May 1943, accompanied by Chinese members of Force 136. Leaving men ashore to contact the guerrillas, he returned to Ceylon to report that they had successfully landed and would arrange for his own reception. By interrogating the crews of junks in the Straits, Davis knew the danger and difficulty facing a European, however skilled a linguist, trying to reach the jungle through the coastal plain. It was decided that the next landing should be off Perak, where the guerrillas were most active, and that, with a wireless operator and other members of Force 136, Davis and his party should be met by a junk, land, and make their way inland. The rendezvous with the junk miscarried and so, on 4 August 1943, they went ashore in folding boats without any reception committee. Davis was soon put in touch with MPAJA guerrillas and made his way into the jungle. Hearing that Chapman was still at large, he sent a message asking him to come to join the party.

In September Broome arrived by submarine and this time the recognition signals with a junk worked, perhaps because Davis was there to organise it. A few weeks later Lim Bo Seng landed from a submarine with two radio transmitters of the latest Type B2, which he hid at Jenderata for subsequent collection.

On 30 September the Perak Regiment of the MPAJA sent

Chin Peng to act as liaison officer between the communists and Davis, with instructions to provide a guard for him and his team. Chin Peng spoke good English and was a man of considerable charm and ability. He already knew Chapman and was to forge a bond with Davis which was to prove of great value when the war ended. After the war he became the leader of the Communist Party after the exposure of Lai Tek's treachery. Other arrivals in the Davis camp were Frank Quayle and Chrystal, both of whom also knew Chapman from earlier exploits.

Davis had arranged for some of the Chinese men who landed with him to work in the community as agents, gathering information which would then be reported to Ceylon. Had he been more aware of the animosity of the Chinese in particular towards the Japanese, he would not have bothered to take the risk that they might be detected because the information was available to the guerrillas without any cloak and dagger arrangements. The Japanese captured two of these agents and one of them told the *Kempeitai* everything he knew. The other managed to escape from Ipoh by sliding down a drainpipe from a lavatory, took a taxi to Bidor, and rejoined Davis. Knowing all that had happened since Davis had landed, the Japanese took draconian steps against the villages on the route he had taken inland, and killed their inhabitants. They also started patrolling intensively the plain between the coast and the jungle, making it impossible for Davis or any of his team to keep four planned rendezvous with submarines or for anyone to bring in the radio equipment hidden in Jenderata.

The months which followed were extremely frustrating for

Davis, Broome, and Chapman. They were unable to make contact with Ceylon and were beginning to run short of provisions. On 1 January 1944 Davis met a disguised Lai Tek, along with Chin Peng. Lai Tek was then Secretary-General of the Communist Party. They agreed that they would cooperate in the fight against the Japanese until the end of the war. The British would supply the guerrillas with arms and training and MPAJA Regiments would accept members of Force 136. Although the topic was not discussed, the communists thought that they would be allowed to enter mainline politics after the war, and the British thought that they would regain their position as the dominant power. It was a misunderstanding with unfortunate consequences and both were to be disappointed.

Quayle had joined Davis in March 1944, bringing with him news of another British refugee, the anthropologist Pat Noone. Quayle and Noone had taken refuge with the Perak Regiment of the MPAJA in May 1942 after failing to find their way to Thailand and the death in the jungle of six British officers who were with them. Both he and Noone became exasperated by the anti-British attitude of the communists and by their emphasis on indoctrination. The two men left the camp together, but soon parted, with Noone saying that he was going to live with the Sakai.

Having nothing better to do and tiring perhaps of the limited company and the inactivity, Chapman decided to set off to track down Noone. He describes his adventures in *The Jungle is Neutral*, including another loss of his diary when he says he was captured by, and escaped from, the Japanese. He stayed with Davis on his return from this escapade until May 1945 when he and Broome were taken to Ceylon by submarine to report upon conditions with the guerrillas and to act as instructors for Force 136. He was still there when the war ended.

Meanwhile, in April 1944, the Japanese had located and attacked Davis's camp, fortunately while he, and other members of his team were away collecting the stores which Lim Bo Seng had hidden in Jenderata, although not the precious radio transmitters. Quayle, who had been left in the camp, managed to escape but all their money, medicine, maps, and other equipment were lost, along, with still more of Chapman's diaries. With every written record made by Chapman in the hands of the Japanese, it is not surprising that some of the dates and detail he gave later are suspect.

Eventually the precious B2 radio transmitters reached Davis. There were endless difficulties associated with providing power for the equipment. Quayle and the radio operator used great ingenuity in trying to convert bicycle-driven car dynamos into power supplies. When helpers from outside the jungle carried in car batteries, they did not always keep them upright, thus losing the acid and the charge. All these problems were overcome by 1 February 1945 and Davis was at last able to talk to Ceylon and arrange the supply of arms for his communist allies and reinforcements for Force 136.

By the end of 1944 the American *Liberator* bomber was in service in India, giving the Royal Air Force the ability to attack Japanese installations in Malaya and Singapore, and to drop men and supplies for the guerrillas. The aircraft first bombed the Singapore naval base on 3 November 1944. Several other raids followed on the island, on port installations in Penang, and on the railway workshops in Kuala Lumpur. After March 1945 the British stopped the bombing because they wanted the port installations to be useable when they invaded.

With free access to Malayan airspace, the *Liberators* were able to drop men and supplies at will. In December 1944 a Malay detachment of Force 136 under Lieutenant-Colonel Debree landed in Upper Perak and established a non-communist and Malay guerrilla force. Similar drops were made in Kedah and Pahang. Before the war ended Force 136 had inserted more than 300 men, of whom less than 100 were British. They had also dropped more than 700 tons of arms and explosives. Only one member of Force 136 lost his life, drowning after landing in water and being unable to disentangle himself from his parachute.

Knowing the intention of the communists to attempt to seize power when the Japanese left, the British were chary about supplying heavy arms to the MPAJA, although there were plenty of rifles, sten guns, PIAT mortars, and explosives. What is certain is that, with at least 2,500 armed and trained men mobilised and three times as many in reserve, the MPAJA would have had no difficulty in blocking the single road and railway linking the eastern states of the peninsula and thus would have played a vital part in helping the invading troops at landing at Morib.

We last saw Maurice Cotterill living on tapioca leaves in a guerrilla band which had been forced to accept four communists to see that they stopped living by robbery and generally behaved themselves. Maurice had refused to leave his companions in the Segamat area to join Chapman. When Davis arrived, Maurice received a suggestion that he should join the rest of the Europeans near Bidor, so that he could be sent by submarine to Ceylon when that was possible. He again refused, largely because, for whatever reason, he had developed a deep distrust for Chapman.

After the low point on the run in 1943, Maurice seems to have had a quiet time so far as attacks from the Japanese or the police were concerned. For a while the guerrillas' diet was inadequate and he continued to suffer from beri-beri. On 19 February 1944 a large party of well-armed communists from Johore joined his group. All was well between the two groups for a few days until, in the middle of the night, the communists rounded up the others, killed 18 of them, and disarmed the others, relegating them to unarmed carriers. Seven of the old gang escaped into the jungle but Maurice sadly recorded that he had lost many good friends. He also noted that the guerrillas were no less ruthless with suspected informers than those in the Regiments with which Chapman and Nona Baker found refuge. Life was not held dear by the MPAJA.

In March 1944, the communists offered to let Maurice move to another camp in North Johore where there were other Europeans in hiding. As he had now been without a British companion for fourteen months, and without any reading matter, he agreed to go. Because he was still suffering from beri-beri which made his feet swell to twice their normal size, the comparatively short journey took five days. He was delighted on arrival to find two Australians called Shepherd and Roach, and Sergeant Stewart, from the Argyll and Sutherland Highlanders, the unit which had fought gallantly and effectively at the time of the invasion. Maurice and the other three were given guard duties by night and by day the chore of grating coconuts to obtain oil. Roach was to die of malaria in April 1945.

The Japanese recognised in 1945 the danger posed by the guerrillas in the event of an invasion and made a major effort to attack the camps. For their part, the MPAJA was becoming bolder in their sorties from the jungle. Maurice reports that his group was attacked several times and had to move camp but without much danger. As he remarked in his diary 'there is nothing done on a large scale'. By the end of the year the Japanese seemed to have given up any hope of eliminating the guerrillas. As a result, early in 1945 the guerrillas no longer bothered to remain in a camp which was hidden from the air, moving into open ground where they could grow sweet potatoes and other vegetables. With more exercise and a better diet, their health quickly improved.

The Johore communists with whom Maurice was living had no Force 136 members attached to keep them in check until the British landed. They derailed two or three trains, assassinated informers and collaborators, harassed public officials, and raided police stations, gathering on one occasion 350 weapons and 20,000 rounds of ammunition. If the Japanese were becoming demoralised, the police were even more so to the extent that they were no longer being used in sweeps against the MPAJA. British planes were flying overhead with impunity and everyone knew that, in Force 136, the British had already returned. For non-combatants, the days of sitting on the fence were coming to an end.

The communists refused to let Maurice, Stewart, and Shepherd leave the jungle until the British had landed at Morib in Selangor. Finally, on 8 September 1945, after 45 months in the jungle, they allowed Maurice to go to Segamat where he met Lieutenant-Colonel Campbell-Miles and his men from Force 136. As he remarks in his diary, he had an excellent reception everywhere. A cynic might have reminded him that the reception the Japanese had received in some quarters in 1942 was not exactly hostile.

We left Nona Baker in the autumn of 1943 living in the one guerrilla camp in Pahang which had not been destroyed by the Japanese, and protected by the communist leader Lao Lee, with whom she and Vincent had earlier gone on the abortive mission to find the stores hidden by Maurice Cotterill, Tyson, and Chiang. She remained in the camp as choir-mistress and kitchen maid. As the months passed, the communists cleared a large area around the camp in which they planted dry rice and other vegetables, including sweet potatoes. Nona hated sweet potatoes and one of her pleasures when the war ended was that she no longer had to pretend that she liked them. With the improved diet her health returned, although she, perhaps fortunately, failed to menstruate the whole time that she was in the jungle.

As elsewhere, Malay police who had worked with the Japanese in Pahang were becoming less enthusiastic in the performance of their duty. Nona was disappointed when, early in 1945, the entire staff of one police station agreed to defect with their arms to the MPAJA, especially as she may have helped influence the decision through her news-sheet. Instead of letting them serve as guerrillas, Lao Lee gave the weapons to his Chinese men and made the policemen work as labourers in the fields. Although she knew of the activities of John Davis and men of

Force 136, her Regiment had no British supervision. They did however acquire an American from the OSS who landed with a transmitter about 100 miles from his planned drop zone and was delivered into the camp. It was he who brought them news of the German surrender.

Using equipment taken from rubber estates, all the Regiments distributed news and propaganda among the civilian population. On one occasion Chapman had been given the chance of preparing an English edition but his second article, on British India, was not to the liking of the communists. Without telling him of their objections, they did not distribute it, and there was no third issue. Nona was more fortunate, or tactful. In January 1945 she had been given the task of preparing an English-language news-sheet which was distributed in the towns and kampongs. Although Lao Lee could not read English, he was delighted with the reception of the paper, despite Nona's insistence on mentioning British successes as well as those of the Russians. Overcoming a desperate shortage of typewriter ribbons and ink for the duplicator, her circulation figure rose during the seven months of publication, from 50 to 70 copies. So popular had her paper, and she herself, become that the communists implored her to stay with them after the war and not return to the British. It was not just a gesture that they had given her a cap of her own with the three red stars.

At the end of August messengers arrived in the camp with instructions for Lao Lee to make his way to Kuantan, taking with him Nona as his English interpreter. After a march of two days, they reached a bungalow on a rubber estate. Japanese soldiers had barricaded themselves in their headquarters in the town and the communists were announcing to everyone that they had won the war and would in future be governing the country. Nona asked if she could go and meet the Europeans who she had heard were now in the vicinity. Her companion put his hand in his pocket and produced a letter addressed to her inviting her to go and join the British until she could obtain a passage back to Britain. The letter was from Colonel Spencer Chapman.

12

Interregnum

When the American Marines captured Iwo Jima in February 1945 after heavy losses and fierce fighting, they denied Japan its principal advance-warning station over which incoming American bombers had to fly. Previous raids had been deadly enough, but at least some of the raiders were shot down. After Iwo Jima the intensified attacks on cities, which were especially prone to damage by incendiary bombs, became even more damaging, causing huge casualties and wide devastation. Without any means of replenishing oil supplies and with industrial production plummeting, no other society except perhaps Nazi Germany would have chosen to continue a war which had in effect long been lost. The Emperor and his closest advisers had known since Midway that at some stage they must concede defeat, but they refused to consider unconditional surrender, with all that implied for the imperial throne.

On 12 July 1945, Hirohito, seeking any way out of the impasse, asked Konoye to instruct Ambassador Sato in Moscow to contact Molotov, on the eve of his departure for the Potsdam conference, to see if, with Soviet help, Japan could obtain any peace terms other than unconditional surrender. Sato cabled back that there was no chance of doing a deal with the Russians. 'Japan is defeated,' he said. 'We must face the fact and act accordingly.' On 2 August Tojo, as Foreign Minister, again pressed Sato to see Molotov, who was then on his way back from Potsdam. Knowing what was about to happen, Molotov replied on 6 August that he would grant Sato an interview two days later. It was on 6 August 1945 that the first atom bomb was dropped and Hiroshima was obliterated.

Two days later a second American plane armed with an atom bomb headed for Kokura, a city of 170,000 inhabitants on the island of Kyushu, to the south of Honshu. Even though it was a clear day, industrial smoke concealed the arms factory which was the aiming point and primary target. Flying onwards, the bombardier briefly had a clear view of Nagasaki. Released from 11,000 feet, the bomb on its parachute drifted off course to the Urakami Valley, which housed the Mitsubishi Ordnance Works. Geography saved Nagasaki from the full destruction of Hiroshima, although the numbers of its dead in the next six months totalled more than 39,000. After Nagasaki Hirohito knew that he had to surrender, whatever the consequences.

Although Lord Louis Mountbatten, the British commander in Southeast Asia, had been told about the atom bomb, the sudden ending of the war meant that his staff were unready to take economic control of the countries for which they now became responsible. To administer Burma, Thailand, Indochina, Hong Kong, Malaya, Borneo, Sarawak, and the Netherlands East Indies, Mountbatten could call on the expertise of less than 140 civilians, most of whom were unfamiliar with local conditions and had received only rudimentary training. Ralph Hone, the official-in-charge of the Malayan Planning Unit, who had in effect been given the task of governing Malaya and Singapore when retaken, had never been there, spoke no Malay or Mandarin, and had scant previous administrative experience. As all the British public officials with relevant knowledge of the peninsula had been interned by the Japanese, Hone and his staff were unprepared for the tasks ahead.

Militarily, Mountbatten was in a slightly stronger position, although here too he had concerns. The Indian troops who had fought gallantly, successfully, and loyally in the Anglo/Indian 14th Army could no longer to be expected to show the same zeal in the suppression of nationalist movements in Indochina, Burma, and the East Indies, although in the event the Divisions given that task performed these disagreeable duties to the best of their ability. Indian Divisions incorporated some British Regiments and the officers of Indian regiments were both Indian and British. This had no effect either way on their loyalty or efficiency. Like their Indian colleagues, few British conscript soldiers were interested in perpetuating the Indian Empire or in restoring colonial rule by force. It was of more concern that demobilisation of British soldiers who had served since 1939 had started in July 1945, and long-serving veterans were being replaced, if at all, by newer and less experienced recruits whose chief wish was to return unharmed to civilian life as soon as possible.

The re-conquest of Malaya and Singapore was to be achieved mainly through a seaborne landing at Morib Beach in Selangor (Operation Zipper). A simultaneous landing on the island of Phuket (designated by some wag as Operation Roger) remains shrouded in mystery to this day. Although the Emperor announced the surrender on 15 August, the Japanese commanders in Singapore did not finally cease military operations in the peninsula until 25 August. To complicate matters further, the Supreme Allied Commander, Douglas

MacArthur, decreed that no Japanese-held territory should be re-occupied until he had taken a formal surrender of Japan in person in Tokyo Bay. Scheduled for 28 August, this event, at which the wretched figure of General Percival made his last formal appearance, had to be postponed until 2 September because of a typhoon.

In fact, the two Indian Divisions destined for the Morib beach from Vizagapatam, Madras, and Rangoon could not have got there much quicker. Some of their ships were already being loaded on 8 August and minesweepers did not leave Colombo to clear the Straits of Malacca until 18 August. There was thus a period of three weeks or more during which all parties in the peninsula could play for position: for the Japanese it was a chance to destroy incriminating evidence; for the Indians to discard their INA uniforms and return to into civilian life; for the Sikh and Malay police to abandon their posts and try to avoid any MPAJA retribution; for the MPAJA to seize what power and weapons it could; for Bose, who had previously consorted with Hitler and Hirohito, to seek sanctuary with an equal tyrant, Stalin; for the prisoners of war and internees to continue to die for want of medical aid; and for the mass of the population to suffer in the hope of better days ahead.

We have seen how the Secretary-General of the Malayan Communist Party, Lai Tek, influenced events first by betraying the party leaders to the Japanese at the Batu Caves conference and then by reaching a deal through John Davis to co-operate with the British. When Hirohito broadcast that the war was over, Lai Tek instructed the MPAJA not to resist the returning British forces. His order, delivered through Chin Peng, generally obeyed with some reluctance and occasionally ignored, ensured that communists did not oppose militarily the return of the British/Indian forces.

By the summer of 1945 members of Force 136 knew that their communist allies were conducting two operations, one jointly with themselves against the Japanese and the other in preparation for the fight they were planning against the British. Apart from the rhetoric of their daily propaganda, the MPAJA were unable to hide the fact that they were preparing caches of weapons in hidden locations. For their part, the British in Ceylon were doing all they could to sponsor non-communist and non-Chinese guerrilla groups and to restrict to small arms the supply of weapons to the MPAJA. Despite so much double-dealing and mutual distrust, personal relationships between the communists and the members of Force 136 remained cordial as did, most importantly, the mutual trust between John Davis and Chin Peng.

To prevent clashes with the Japanese before the 14th Army arrived, Mountbatten issued a command from distant Ceylon that the MPAJA should keep away from towns and cities which housed Japanese troops until the British took over. John Davis advised him that the order was not only unfair and unenforceable: it was also dangerous because, if they tried to put it into effect, he and his fellow-members of Force 136 would lose whatever control they possessed over the activities of the communists. Mountbatten then amended the order to allow the guerrillas freedom of movement so long as they did not start fighting the Japanese.

Emerging from the jungle, MPAJA guerrillas joined up with

their outside helpers to enjoy their moment of triumph and inflict summary punishment on those who had collaborated with the Japanese and on anyone else they considered a threat. Few if any of the *Kempeitai* on the mainland survived long enough to help the returning British identify those most guilty of what they judged to be war crimes. The degree of MPAJA violence varied in different parts of the country, depending largely upon whether there was the restraining presence of officers from Force 136. In some kampongs they set up 'Peoples' Committees', the apparatus of a totalitarian dictatorship. In the larger towns, Malay civil servants and Chinese *towkays*, people they assumed to have collaborated with the Japanese, became their victims. Everywhere they sought to take control of food stores and fuel supplies, to seize the huge quantities of banana currency printed but not yet issued by the Japanese, to requisition transport, and to collect and conceal arms collected from police stations or Japanese camps.

In Kelantan, which had been one of the states ceded to Thailand and thus become less subject to Japanese military control, a unit of a guerrilla force which called itself the Overseas Chinese Anti-Japanese Army repelled the MPAJA and occupied Kota Bharu. It was accompanied by a British official called J.K. Creer who had spent the war in the jungle. In other districts where there were no communists, armed bands of robbers, often falsely claiming to be MPAJA men, plundered the population. In Singapore a Johore Regiment of the MPAJA started a reign of terror among Chinese business and community leaders. Ostensibly meting out justice to those who had collaborated with the Japanese, the violence in the city, as elsewhere, included the settlement of personal vendettas through denunciation and the elimination of future threats to a Marxist state.

Force 136 had tried to place men with the Pahang regiment of the MPAJA to which Nona Baker belonged by dropping a Malayan game warden called Leonard and a small team with instructions to contact them. Leonard reported back to Ceylon that he and his men were unwelcome and, after the surrender, they remained in Jerantut. On about 1 September Chapman was dropped near Raub in Pahang and on 5 September entered Kuala Lipis, where he received a warm welcome from the Chinese townspeople. He then made his way to Kuantan where, as we saw, he sent a letter to Nona Baker. Although she had heard a rumour that there were British soldiers in the vicinity, her first sight of jungle-green uniforms worn by members of Force 136 was at a Kuantan cinema. The communists had taken over the town and the Japanese were nowhere to be seen. Ominously, Nona had seen her MPAJA companions moving stores of rice into the jungle, to prepare for their next stage of operations against the British.

After meeting Spencer Chapman, who was accompanied by an Australian Major also called Chapman, Nona stayed with the Europeans until she received a message from the MPAJA leader Lao Chuang asking her to visit him. She was advised not to go, knowing the treatment meted out by the communists to possible informers. With some trepidation, she sought out Lao Chuang, whose concern was that she should not tell Spencer Chapman, or indeed anyone else, what he and his people were planning and especially that she should keep quiet about the shifting of stores into the jungle. To that she agreed, and returned safely to the British. Another four weeks were to pass before British troops appeared in strength in Kuantan and displaced the communists.

Although it was outside their sphere of operations, the Americans had sought to infiltrate agents into Malaya, one of whom, as we saw, found his way to Nona Baker's Regiment. In a bizarre exploit sanctioned by Mountbatten, in August they captured and detained the Sultan of Pahang who was travelling to Kuala Lumpur to be crowned king of an independent Malaya. A more serious move towards Malayan independence had been made by Ibrahim Jaacob who led both a political party and a Malay military unit which were supported or tolerated by the Japanese. His aim for a Malay nation which included Sumatra did not appeal to the Sultans, or to the Sumatrans themselves who felt they would have enough on their hands expelling the Dutch without also taking on the British. On 19 August, 1945 Ibrahim left for Jakarta and did not return, leaving other Malays to survive the turmoil of the interregnum as best they could.

The occupation had effected one major change in the attitude of the Indians living in the peninsula. Local volunteers in the Indian National Army included both Tamil rubber tappers, who tended to make up the rank-and-file, and the sons of business and professional men, who became officers and received Japanese military training. For the first time, both classes made common cause in their fight against British imperialism and, although they were eventually disillusioned by the Japanese, the mutual understanding and collaboration between Indians from different backgrounds remained a new political factor. The Indian Government set up by Bose in the

Andaman and Nicobar Islands did not survive the surrender, despite being recognised by the Irish President de Valera in a gesture almost as strange as his formal expression of regret to Nazi Germany on the death of Hitler. Although Nehru and the Congress Party in India had changed its policy about the Indian National Army from condemnation in 1942 to approval in 1945, the death of Bose in a plane crash on his way to Moscow came as a relief to other people than the British.

Small detachments of British troops landed in Penang and Singapore a few days earlier than the Morib landings, but the interregnum only ended with the arrival of the British/Indian troops in Selangor on 9 September 1945. Many myths have been created and repeated about Morib, based in part on a report circulated by 224 Group of the Royal Air Force. The view from the air was clearly different from that on the ground. Only one field gun was lost, after its tractor stalled in the sea and a landing craft hit it before the tractor, limber, and gun could be winched out. Unlike the Japanese experience at Kota Bharu, all the tanks and sift-skinned vehicles got ashore. None of the landing craft became stranded on the beach, although there were a number of 'dry' landings, when the craft stayed on the sand when the tide went out to facilitate unloading. The advantage of Morib was that the Japanese did not anticipate a landing there. There were no beach defences and no more than 1,000 troops close enough to react quickly to the landing. The disadvantages were that the sand was soft, so that many vehicles needed winching out of the surf, and that there was only one road leading inland from the beach which, as in the Normandy landings, caused bottlenecks.

The Japanese had decided not to oppose any landing on the beaches. Like the British in 1941, they were defending the country with three Divisions. Expecting the invasion to come through Thailand or Kedah, their main strength was based in the north of the peninsula, although they had moved the 37th Division into Johore from Java. They had also transferred troops from Indochina. In total, their own fighting strength numbered around 125,000 men. Although the majority of its force had deserted, been killed, or been captured in Burma, the Indian National Army still had in Malaya between 15,000 and 20,000 men. The Japanese considered them unreliable and, if the Burmese experience were to be repeated, they were right.

Having resisted previously the temptation to ponder on what might have happened in hypothetical circumstances, we need not conjecture what the outcome of the invasion might have been if the atom bombs had not been dropped. Suffice it to say that the position of 1941 as between the combatants was almost exactly reversed. The British now commanded the sea and the air. The Japanese High Command had conceded in its planning that it could not hold Malaya and anticipated at best a withdrawal down the peninsula to Syonan-to, light of the south (soon again to become Singapore), where they would fight to the last. The British/Indian forces came after a stream of victories, and those units which had not been in action previously were studded with men who had. The Japanese were poorly trained, had low morale, and one of their Divisions consisted of older conscripts who had not seen action. When they invaded in 1941, the Japanese received help from some of the population and acceptance by others. By 1945, virtually every hand was turned against them. General Slim said the invasion would have succeeded and, almost alone among British generals, he always won his battles.

Maurice Cotterill was obliged to stay with the guerrillas until 13 September. Contrary to press reports, he was physically in good health although, as with other British fugitives, the traumata arising from his years of danger, malnutrition, illness, and isolation would take many years to heal, and the scars would never totally vanish. He went first to Jasin in Malacca, where the army used him as a liaison officer with the MPAJA, and then to Malacca town. He says in his diary that everyone seemed happy that the British were back, which may also have reflected their relief that the Japanese were gone and their hopes for a rapid improvement in their condition. On 18 September he went to Kuala Lumpur to arrange a passage back to Britain and on 27 September he left Singapore, leaving the task of restoring order out of chaos to the ill-prepared officials and soldiers of the British Military Administration.

13

Desolation and Recovery

Maurice Cotterill sailed from Singapore to Britain in the autumn of 1945. The only possessions he retained from before the war were some letters from his mother, which survive to this day. His journey took him past an empire which still circled the globe but was in the process of collapse. Appearances were deceptive. British forces occupied most of the countries he passed by but in some they were faced with seemingly insuperable problems, nor could the British economy support their ongoing cost.

To the north of Malaya in Indochina, General Gracey's 20th Indian Division found itself trying to hold the ring between confident nationalists and the numerous French colonists, who until March that year, as adherents to Vichy, had not been treated by the Japanese as enemy aliens. When General Leclerc arrived under instructions from de Gaulle to restore colonial rule, Mountbatten warned him against extremist policies. 'I have my orders,' Leclerc replied. The consequence of those orders was decades of bloodshed leading to ultimate humiliation for the French and Americans.

In Indonesia General Christison's 23rd Indian Division was facing an equally difficult task. Before the British successfully bombed Sumatra's oil refinery, which had been of critical importance to Tokyo's conduct of the war, most Dutch internees had not been rigorously controlled by the Japanese. Following the bombing and as the Japanese fortunes waned, the Dutch were more harshly treated. In the chaos surrounding the abrupt ending of the war, the colonists were generally much fitter than those who had been interned in Singapore. Once free, they sought to turn the clock back to 1942 while the nationalists, well armed but initially ill-organised, fought for independence.

The 25th Indian Division in Thailand faced fewer problems. As with their French neighbours, when Japanese defeat loomed, the government in Bangkok decided to rethink its allegiance and the Regent contacted the British in secret to facilitate their arrival. As we noted, one of Thailand's first actions after the war was to return to Malaya the four states which the Japanese had handed over as a reward for Thai help in 1941.

Maurice Cotterill's route home took him past Burma, India, and Ceylon, all finding their way to independence with varying degrees of internal conflict, confusion, and unrest and calling for yet more British troops on the ground to maintain order, if not the perpetuation of imperial rule. As he passed across the Indian Ocean, to his right lay Iraq and Iran, both secured from Axis control in 1941 by Slim's 10th Indian Division in lightning campaigns as conclusive as the Division's defeat of pro-Axis French forces in Syria. These countries also needed British garrisons. Most liners stopped to refuel in Aden, where British rule was not yet challenged, before proceeding to the Suez Canal. Egypt still housed British troops, who were facing rioters in Cairo protesting against their presence and against Jewish immigration into Palestine.

In Palestine, British forces were being attacked by both Jews and Arabs. In Greece, the army was engaged in combating a communist coup. In Italy, the units in Trieste were facing down a threat from Tito's Yugoslavia. Other soldiers and airmen were occupying Libya, Austria, and Germany, quite apart from those stationed in colonies round the world. Britain had been able to retain its empire so long as its subjects consented to the rule, but when consent was withdrawn, the empire collapsed.

Arriving in Britain, Maurice found a society for which the transient joy of victory could not offset the physical and emotional damage wrought by six years of conflict and family separation. Towns and cities had been bombed and, even where the devastation had been tidied up, buildings had not been replaced. Manufacturing industry, mobilised for war, was faced with re-inventing itself and its products for peacetime. Females had been conscripted for essential work just as males were for the armed services. As soon as the regulations were eased, many women chose to leave their uncongenial jobs in manufacturing industry and transport. Many returning conscripts might be able to fill unskilled jobs but for six years, apprenticeships, tertiary education, and other professional training had been neglected. There was inevitably a shortage of skilled workers and managers.

Food, clothing, furniture, and fuel were rationed while other necessities, including housing or cars, were in short supply or unobtainable. Freed from wartime restrictions on strikes and faced with continued inflation, trade unions showed a militancy which took no account of the national economic woes. The week that Maurice landed in Britain, 43,000 dockers went on strike to obtain a national minimum wage of 25 shillings a day.

Britain had entered the war as a prosperous nation with substantial financial reserves and assets. When in 1941 these had been exhausted buying arms from the United States,

President Roosevelt introduced the policy of lend-lease, enabling the supply of weapons to continue, the British to survive, and the United States to prosper. Truman ended lend-lease abruptly when the fighting stopped. Before the war, Malaya had been, even with its exports of tin, rubber, iron ore, bauxite, and timber, a relatively minor contributor to Britain's world trade, accounting to about one fortieth of the whole. In 1945, with dollar reserves exhausted and the deficit continuing to mount, politicians and civil servants in London eagerly sought to garner whatever benefit they could from any quarter and especially from Malaya, a territory which had always and almost uniquely been a consistent economic contributor to the sterling area.

The plan to convert the Malay states into a single British colony independent of Singapore was hatched in London before the war ended and announced in the House of Commons on 10 October 1945. A British special representative, Harold MacMichael, who had formerly been High Commissioner in Palestine, had arrived in Malaya three days earlier to persuade or coerce the Sultans to accede to the plan, which involved the surrender of their independence and the repudiation by the British of previous treaties. The Sultans felt themselves in no position to negotiate. Only five of the nine had been on the throne in 1941 and the other four sought British recognition of their legitimacy. Nobody had forgotten their obeisance to Yamashita in April 1942, or their demeanour with Tojo in July 1943. Those with longer memories may have pondered on the outcome of the disputed succession in Perak in 1874, which gave the British the chance to secure political and economic control over Malaya's richest state.

By Christmas, 1945, all the Sultans had signed. Their acceptance of the plan, which they were to try to repudiate three months later, caused outrage among their Malay subjects and little enthusiasm among other communities. MacMichael's influence on the future of Malaysia was not all bad. The concept of a single nation state in the peninsula, separated from Singapore, became a reality. Faced with the assault on their ancient laws and customs, growing political consciousness among Malays led to the formation of a Malay political party which would ultimately develop into the movement which negotiated freedom. Those of Chinese and Indian descent also identified themselves as citizens of their country of domicile rather than expatriates. As for the communists, on 7 November Lai Tek added self-government to the 'eight principles' which he had previously laid down, leading in due time to all parties expressing the same aim.

From his lair in Britain, Frank Swettenham fulminated at the British breach of faith. He had also to remind the newspaper that he was not in fact dead, as a previous correspondent had suggested.

In retrospect, it seems surprising that such a plan should have been formulated by a socialist government, however short of foreign currency, without prior consultation with those affected or consideration of the changes brought about by the Japanese occupation. Prime Minister Attlee and his team retained a prewar British concept of the inability of less developed peoples to govern themselves Britain had a paternal duty to its colonial empire which they intended to discharge. Mountbatten, who was on good personal terms with nationalist leaders in India and Burma, was more realistic. He expressed his reservations to London about the MacMichael plan but was overruled.

The fact was that Malays, who had administered the country under the Japanese in difficult circumstances, knew that they were capable of governing without British supervision or intervention. Those of Indian and Chinese descent living in the peninsula, unable to leave during the war, had ceased to be a transient population and were raising families whose home was Malaya. We have noted already the influence of the Indian National Army and the squatter phenomenon. The greatest factor in the changed situation, however, was the status of the white man. In 1942 the British had been crushed by an inferior number of Asiatics. While the Chinese had fought, the British had surrendered. The myth or image of European supremacy had been destroyed. It was a factor which had failed to register with the politicians in London, or indeed with many of the internees themselves. The soldiers on the spot knew differently.

As with the Morib landing, so the performance of the British Military Administration (BMA) between September 1945 and March 1946 has been subject to adverse comment by those who were, of necessity, not there at the time and accept the version of events put about by those who came after. An announcement made in leaflets dropped before the landing decreed the demonetisation of the Japanese banana currency. This decision affected mainly poor people and was taken with reservations at the Bank of England, despite the fact that the banana notes had no backing. The dollar issued by the Japanese had long been suspect, as was shown when a sliding scale was finally adopted for the purpose of paying compensation to some of those who had suffered from the demonetisation. It had held its own with the Straits dollar until January 1943. By January 1944, $1 Straits was worth $4.55 banana. By January, 1945 the ratio was 20 to one. On the eve of demonetisation, 12 August 1945, $100 Straits was equal to $95,000 banana.

Because the Straits dollars had commanded a premium, the banana currency had ceased to circulate. Wealthy people had hoarded them and, on the first day a Chinese bank re-opened its doors in Penang, it received around $50,000 in deposits of Straits currency. The MPAJA were especially indignant about the demonetisation. During the interregnum, they had seized huge quantities of the banana currency, although they failed to find a room stacked with cases containing notes of all denominations in the guardroom at one of the Japanese camps at Bidor in Perak.

For three or four weeks, the absence of cash as a medium of exchange caused difficulties for the BMA as it did for local inhabitants, cigarettes providing a temporary substitute for dollars. To get notes into circulation quickly, the soldiers of the BMA were told to engage as many workers as they could, preferably in jobs which would help the economy recover but, if no project were available, on any task which would justify payment of a living wage. Glyn Gabe, a Captain stationed with the Royal Devon Yeomanry at Ipoh who was a Chartered Surveyor in civilian life, employed dozens of workers of all races on road clearance and weeding overgrown rubber estates, paying them weekly with cash he drew from the bank authenticated by thumb prints. As the Gabe thumb regularly had to come into play to balance accounts, there were plenty of opportunities for cheating in someone less honest than Captain Gabe. Other people were found employment in non-essential tasks such as renovating the golf course in the Cameron Highlands or as stable boys at the Perak Turf Club. One Battery of the Yeomanry, stationed in the comfortable billet of the Majestic Hotel, engaged the entire hotel staff at public expense, although they continued to enjoy Hard-living Allowance and Japanese Campaign Pay from a generous paymaster in India.

It was important that the banking system should function normally as soon as possible. Those banks which had continued to operate under the occupation re-opened their doors on 17 September 1945. The Mercantile Bank in Singapore opened a day earlier. The Chartered Bank and the Hong Kong Bank were also quickly back in business in Singapore, Kuala Lumpur, Malacca, and other cities. Their prewar staff immediately reported for duty and in Singapore they discovered that Mutoh had kept his word about their records, although gold and precious stones had been taken from the vaults.

The BMA instructed the banks to give credit freely to all business, whether controlled by Europeans or local businessmen. Although the big three British banks did not restart operations in Ipoh until 1946, another officer from the Yeomanry, Frank Bedder, who was a Chartered Accountant, worked with the bankers to see that their normal caution was replaced by unwonted generosity. Those with whom he associated repaid his help by running the Tote at the popular race meeting held by the Regiment on Boxing Day, 1945.

There were, however, even more serious matters to attend to before worrying about how to get $160 million of notes into circulation quickly. Those who looked to the army for an instant increase in the availability of rice were disappointed. The best it could do was ensure that stores seized by the communists in the interregnum were made available to all. It was beyond the army's power to increase the import of rice beyond what was available from traditional sources in Burma or Thailand. Corn imports from the United States were slow to arrive and did not prove an acceptable substitute. Although the shortage of food was the most urgent issue, leading to unfair criticism of the BMA, almost every other household commodity was also missing from the shelves except, perhaps, Kiwi shoe polish. Those who had abandoned their vegetable plots were urged to keep cultivating them. The speed at which the economy recovered in the next few months, despite the problems in finding rice to import, was a testimony to the industry and ingenuity of the local population, but it also owed something to the efforts of the maligned BMA.

The entire infrastructure of the country had been neglected during the occupation that led to a decline in health standards. The Royal Engineers undertook the urgent task of repairing sewage systems. Fitters from the Royal Electrical and Mechanical Engineers repaired damaged power equipment and restored electricity supply. Solicitors became magistrates and judges. Teachers helped schools return to normal. A Regiment consisting of British soldiers such as that stationed in Ipoh consisted of 99 per cent conscripts, among whom every trade and skill could be discovered, including a circus boy to look after the racehorses. All these men with skills were seconded to civilian duties.

The record of the BMA was patchy because Indian Regiments, who formed the majority, consisted of professional officers and soldiers who had no other training. In Batu Gajah, for example, Indian soldiers undertook few of the civilian duties carried out by their British neighbours in Ipoh because they had nobody with relevant skills or experience. The Yeomanry were able to meet the demands on their men from Ipoh, the Cameron Highlands, and Kuala Kangsar but demobilisation made it increasingly difficult to answer the calls for help which reached them from Taiping and other Perak towns. There were inevitably ample opportunities for dishonesty, and not all of them were passed by. For all that, the economic record of the BMA was, in the circumstances, much better than could have been expected given the short notice at which it was performed.

Another duty which faced the BMA was the disarming, processing, and delivery to Singapore of Japanese surrendered personnel. In the area commanded by Moutbatten, there were 482,000 Japanese soldiers when the war ended, of whom over 125,000 were stationed in Malaya. The BMA had no local information about the numbers and location of these men nor any food for them to eat. A small unit sent to deal with a camp near Bidor in Perak discovered several hundred Japanese, many of them burdened with loot they had brought with them from Indochina. Some prisoners had handed their weapons to, or been disarmed by, the MPAJA in the interregnum. By October all had been disarmed, relieved of their booty, and sent to Singapore for onward dispatch to Rempang Island and Japan—apart from the 39,000 who were kept back to do manual work.

Although many of the *Kempeitai* had been killed by the MPAJA before the British returned, there was no shortage of other Japanese and their Korean vassals who were considered to have committed war crimes. The tribunals established in Singapore, Kuala Lumpur, Penang, and Seremban sentenced a great number to death on evidence which might not stand up in a normal jurisdiction, but most of their victims were not around to testify. Many of the death sentences were not carried out but 199 men were executed, and 126 imprisoned. General Yamashita was tried in Manila and hanged on 23 February 1946.

The soldiers of the BMA took a pragmatic view about charges of collaboration by civilians with the Japanese. The sooner the police and civil servants returned to duty, the more quickly the economy would recover. The issue of the Indian National Army seemed to incense Indian officers more than it did their British colleagues. It seemed unimportant that many shopkeepers chose to keep a picture of Bose in the window except for those Indian soldiers who took seriously the oath they had taken when they joined the army and despised those who had broken it.

A BMA regimental Commanding Officer's instructions were short and to the point. He was to prevent disorder and safeguard the health of the population. Communal strife was the concern of the BMA only if it led to violence. The army had no instructions to deal with squatters. Apart from a Sunday morning meeting of Commanding Officers to discuss their mutual problems, and solutions to those problems, few orders and scant advice reached them from Kuala Lumpur or

Singapore. They imposed no censorship nor any restriction on public meeting. Those given the task of patrolling the countryside to prevent looting or smuggling were told that on no account should they injure of kill anyone. If fired at, they should either not fire back, or aim to miss. In the five months of its rule, the BMA turned out to be the most liberal form of government ever seen in the peninsula before or since, and led to the artistic outburst known as the Malayan Spring.

The British BMA soldiers differed from other Europeans working in Malaya in that they had little aspiration to racial superiority. When Mrs Edith Rattray, who owned the Green Cow Tavern in the Cameron Highlands, declined to be repatriated to Britain and found her way to Tapah Road railway station at the end of September 1945, she was affronted that the army had failed within two weeks of the landing to institute a bus service to the Highlands. Greig Barr, the young Commanding Officer of the Royal Devon Yeomanry, fed her, gave her a bed for the night, and sent her up the hill by jeep next day. Her words at dinner remained graven in his memory 60 years later. Her first night in prison the Japanese had put her in a cell with a 'coolie woman. They never made that mistake again.' Those who had served with Indian troops or in a West African Division did not think of people in terms of 'coolies'.

British soldiers were soon to discover that Mrs Rattray's attitude towards other races was not exceptional among officials returning to duty in Malaya after years of confinement. Imprisonment appeared to have created for some a time warp, a Rip Van Winkle effect. The soldiers also, as the months passed, detected a change in the attitude of the Chinese population in the countryside as the communists extended their control, and especially among the squatters who rightly feared eviction. The Indians on the estates were also unfriendly if not actively hostile. Only the Malays and urban Chinese retained a neutral attitude towards the imperial soldiers.

Lai Teck had agreed to the standing down of the MPAJA and on 1 December 1945 parades were held, medals handed out, weapons surrendered, and a bounty of $350 paid to each man, of which the communist party took $100. Officers in the BMA knew that the communists were still collecting weapons from Japanese arsenals and that trouble was brewing. However, on All Fool's Day in 1946, they once again became no more than conscript soldiers, anxiously awaiting demobilisation and praying not to be posted to Java.

The previous month, in March 1946, Maurice Cotterill had married Sybil Kendrick in Britain and then accepted a job on a rubber estate in Borneo. He was to return in 1949 to the estate at Kuala Reman, where he had worked before the war. Two previous managers had been murdered by the Malayan Peoples' Anti-British Army, led by John Davis's old friend, Chin Peng.

14

Conflict and Independence

The MacMichael plan had one merit. It addressed the vexed question of the right to citizenship of other races than Malays who lived in the peninsula and Singapore. In the census taken in 1941, there were 2,418,665 Chinese, 2,268,581 Malays, 717,693 Indians, 34,231 Europeans, and 80,035 others. The number of the *orang asli*, the original inhabitants living in the jungle, was not recorded but was estimated to be around 40,000. A relatively small number of Malays were immigrants from Sumatra. Slightly less than half the Chinese had been born abroad and many would have intended to return to China when their employment ended. Tamils also, who worked on the rubber estates, might return to India. With very few exceptions, the Europeans were expatriates. The European people were by no means all British and, as we noted previously, in 1941 there had been some 6,000 Japanese residents whose mass departure that autumn would have put on guard a more acute observer than Air Chief Marshal Brooke-Popham.

Just as the Chinese came from different regions and spoke dialects which were in effect different languages, so their activities covered a wide spectrum. The *towkay*, planter, miner, artisan, and businessman formed the commercial heart of the community. Immigrant Chinese wage-earners, who before the war worked in the tin and rubber industries, had during the occupation out of necessity become growers of food on land which had been formerly jungle fringe or part of an estate.

Labelled squatters, these people numbered in 1945 between 400,000 and 500,000. Most of them had achieved, for the first time, a stake in the land and their food production had become vital to the whole community. Unlike many prewar workers, they also had wives and children living with them. When, after 1945, many of the squatters resumed paid employment, they were no longer solely dependant on the weekly wage packet and therefore in a stronger bargaining position with their employers, whether European and Chinese.

The Malays, during the occupation, had demonstrated their administrative ability. More than half of those who later became Ministers in the Federal Government, including Tunku Abdul Rahman himself, had worked in the civil service. They also formed the core of the farming community and were less engaged in paid employment than the Chinese or Tamils. For social and religious reasons, the majority did not wish to see any change in the status of the Sultans. Although they were just outnumbered by immigrant workers, they did not accept that other races should have equal political rights with themselves or that regions reserved for their exclusive use should be opened up to others. Some political activists aspired to a union of Malay peoples which would embrace Sumatra but, as we saw, that desire was not reciprocated in what was about to become the state of Indonesia.

The Indian population had declined dramatically during the occupation, partly because many who joined the Indian National Army did not return and also because of the death rate of Tamil labourers on the Burma railway. On one Selangor estate, for example, 68 out of 70 men conscripted were lost. The

Indians, like the Chinese, did not form a cohesive community although they were united in their rejection of British imperialism whether in the sub-continent or in the peninsula. As with Chinese wage-earners, after the war the tappers ceased being a complaisant workforce in what had previously been a semi-feudal system. Indian traders and shopkeepers, most of whom had enthusiastically backed Bose, could be expected to support any party which had the aim of achieving independence from Britain.

The British in Malaya, while jealous of their political control when other colonial powers came snooping, had never sought exclusivity in business. Apart from the dominance of the Chinese in the commercial life of Malaya and Singapore, there had been no bar to traders of other nationalities. We have already noted that in 1941 the three British banks had French, Dutch, Japanese, Indian, American, and many Chinese competitors. As in Burma after 1945, the British were more concerned about the stability of a country in which they retained substantial commercial interests than in seeking a dominant trading position. They also wanted to keep Malaya's dollar earnings within the embattled sterling area.

Very few British people settled in Malaya. Although it was described as a British colony, the British were not colonists in the sense that the Malays themselves had once been and many of the Chinese and Indians still were. Malaya was also unusual in that, unlike much of the world, the infrastructure had been developed, but had never been owned, by the British. London had, for example, financed the building of railways in India and South America and thereafter retained ownership of companies which operated them. In Malaya, thanks in large part to Swettenham, the infrastructure had been paid for through taxation and was owned by the state.

As MacMichael had demonstrated, it was going to be hard enough to reconcile all the conflicting interests in a new constitution without any further complication. That was not to be. The world was entering the era of the Cold War and even before Lai Tek had been exposed and killed in Bangkok in 1947, Chin Peng and the communists had continued working to establish in Malaya a Marxist totalitarian state such as those already taking shape elsewhere under Russian sponsorship. It was to be a struggle for which the British and the Malayan people were ill-prepared.

In the wake of the MacMichael diktat, on 1 March 1946 the representatives of over 40 Malay organisations met in Kuala Lumpur to discuss their political future. Observing the slaughter of aristocrats in Java and Sumatra, the delegates rejected any policy which might encourage egalitarian excess in Malaya. With sporadic communal violence rife between Malays and Chinese, villagers and townspeople alike wanted security. The meeting was momentous because it led to the formation of the United Malays National Organisation (UMNO) under the leadership of a Johore aristocrat and Minister, Dato' Onn bin Jaafar. Onn was still leader when the unpopular Malayan Union was replaced by the more broadly-based Federation of Malaya in February 1948. By 1951, however, his behaviour had became unpredictable and eccentric. He declared himself against immediate independence from Britain and, in an equally damaging switch of policy, turned against the Sultans.

Onn's unlikely, but inspired, successor was a Cambridge-educated aristocrat, Tunku Abdul Rahman, whose knowledge of the classics acquired in that seat of learning was not thought to extend beyond the Derby, the St Leger, the Oaks, and the Two Thousand Guineas. Yet the Tunku, despite the civil war waged by the communists, proved the man to square the circle, reconciling all interests except those who sought to establish a totalitarian People's Republic, such as those in North Korea or eastern Europe. In 1952 he formed an alliance with the Malayan Chinese Association, which provided stability and leadership to the Malaysian people for the next six decades. The manoeuvres and switched allegiances of other politicians and parties during this period, recorded in detail by learned historians, may be likened to the movement of bobbins on a braiding machine, which pirouette around each other until finally a cord stronger than the sum of the individual components emerges. So it was with UMNO.

It is hard today, for those who have seen the oppression inherent in the maintenance of power by a Marxist regime and the failure of command economies, to understand the attraction which communism held for so many people in 1945. Certainly the Soviet people had fought with great gallantry after Stalin's alliance with Hitler was shattered by Barbarossa. There was a belief, and not just among idealistic social scientists, in Asia as in Europe, that private wealth was wicked and individual freedom under capitalism had failed. In Malaya the communists had won prestige through their resistance to the Japanese. They hoped to win power without resort to arms, but, if force were necessary, they were ready to use it.

The tactics of the Malayan Communist Party (MCP), dominated by ex-MPAJA men, were to make the country ungovernable by destroying the economy through control of the trade unions, building also on the *min yuen*. From London the Labour government, itself the political arm of a trade union movement, sought to encourage unions in Singapore and the peninsula and, despite growing disorder and intimidation, discouraged the Governor from imposing any restrictions on their activity. In 1945 a British union official, John Brazier, arrived as an adviser to foster union membership. Brazier was steeped in a trade union tradition which had not involved cutting the fingers off rubber tappers who ignored an instruction to strike or the murder of those who opposed recruitment. Despite, or perhaps partly because of, Brazier's sponsorship of moderates, by the end of 1946 the communists had obtained control of the unions representing both Chinese and Indian workers. In the year following the ending of the BMA on 1 April 1946, almost 2,900,000 working days were lost through strikes in Malaya and Singapore.

Although in February 1947 the MCP had only 11,000 Chinese members, 700 who were Indians, and even fewer Malays, its support throughout the country was not based only on the unions and the *min yuen*. At some stage the government would have to decide what to do about the mainly Chinese squatters who had colonised the jungle fringe and occupied part of many rubber estates. These people had fed the MPAJA during the occupation and many of them looked upon the communists as their natural protectors.

Faced with economic chaos through incessant strikes, in

1947 the government introduced legislation banning trade unions from political action. It proved a dead letter. The liberal but indecisive Governor, Edward Gent, drew back from giving the police the powers they needed to deal with the mounting violence. John Dalley, the experienced police officer who had led the valiant Dalforce in 1942, resigned in exasperation at Gent's dithering and obduracy. With the government losing control, in March 1948 the MCP leadership met and decided on military action. On 10 May it met again and decided to start the war in September 1948. The March plenum also decreed that all strike-breakers should be killed— another departure from the custom and practice with which the trade union adviser, John Brazier, had been familiar back home.

Gent had some excuse for acting cautiously. In the summer of 1948 there were very few troops in the country and the police were still recovering from the damage caused by their activities under the Japanese. No longer able to call on the services of the Indian army, which was now divided between India and Pakistan and threatening to go to war under its two British Commanders-in-Chief over Kashmir, the troops consisted of two British battalions, six Regiments of Ghurkhas, and three of Malays. There was also one Regiment of the Royal Artillery, which was of little use in jungle warfare. The police numbered around 10,000 with another 12,000 auxiliaries. The intelligence arm of the police was equally unready. It lacked Chinese speakers and was in no position to provide the information without which the uprising could not be put down.

In December 1947, 151 squatters in Sungei Siput had been prosecuted for occupying land without permits. Armed with court orders, bailiffs pulled up their crops and destroyed their houses. Although rice production was approaching prewar levels, other foods produced by the squatters formed an important part of a still meagre public diet. The Sungei Siput area had a history of disaffection and the deeply unpopular moves against the squatters were the trigger that started the shooting. On 16 June 1948 the decision by the MCP to commence military operations in September was pre-empted in Sungei Siput by the murder of three British rubber planters. Following a subsequent attack on a police station in Johore, the following week a State of Emergency was proclaimed throughout Malaya.

In the next few days, the police managed to arrest many of the activists of the MCP but, despite being taken by surprise, some 2,000 guerrillas, including Chin Peng, made their way into the jungle to prepared camps. Their call for old comrades from the MPAJA to join them fell to a large extent on deaf ears. Many former guerrillas had been refugees from the Japanese rather than ardent communists. They had settled down with their families and did not relish a return to the rigours of life in the jungle. There was, however, for some years no shortage of recruits, some actuated by political conviction and others by the prospect of the excitement of guerrilla life.

For three years the British seemed unable to make headway against the insurrection. National Servicemen sent from Britain lacked motivation and training, and proved poor soldiers. The nadir seemed to have been reached on 6 October 1951 when the High Commissioner, Henry Gurney, was killed in an ambush on the road to Fraser's Hill. General Briggs, a forceful and thoughtful army commander, was about to retire. William Jenkins, who had been responsible for the Intelligence Branch was dismissed, and on 1 December Nicol Gray, the Commissioner of Police, resigned. There was thus at the end of the year no High Commissioner, Police Commissioner, or Chief of the Intelligence Branch.

Appearances were deceptive. The guerrillas had greater problems. Although given a boost in 1950 by the British government's recognition of the communist government in China, they received no assistance from overseas. Their excesses during the interregnum had not been forgotten and a continued policy of extortion and terrorism alienated the population. The slashing of rubber trees so that they would not for many years produce latex damaged the economy but it also threw tappers out of work. When trains were derailed, innocent citizens rather than soldiers or police died or were wounded. So great was the public disaffection with the communists, or the Malayan Races Liberation Army, as it was now called, that, when in 1950 volunteers were called for among the civil population to enlist in defence organisations, half a million people offered their services. Before the Emergency ended, 300,000 armed members of the Home Guard, first established by Briggs in December 1949, defended their own kampongs. By then 2,590 police, 3,253 civilians, 518 servicemen, and 99 European planters had lost their lives.

Apart from trying to kill the guerrillas, the methods adopted by Briggs included amnesties, rewards for information and surrender, internment of suspected subversives, and propaganda. He also planned to clear the country progressively from the south by starving them out. A combination of identity cards, rationing, puncturing of tins of produce when they were sold, communal feeding, and defoliation of jungle cultivation proved only partly effective To make the starvation policy work, it was also necessary to stop the guerrillas obtaining food from the *orang asli* and the squatters. By 1950 the number of squatters had fallen to a hardcore of about 150,000. Their forced and initially badly-organised relocation to areas inaccessible to the communists led to great hardship, especially among the 20,000 *orang asli* who were so treated. The deportation of up to 35,000 squatters who were unable to produce any documentation—men, women, and children—to an uncertain fate in China was equally cruel.

Using extortion and terror, Chin Peng had plenty of money but insufficient food. He was able to keep together small bands of guerrillas for local attacks and assassinations but could not maintain and feed a sufficient number to threaten the army or to retain control of a 'liberated area'. Facing a stalemate or defeat in Malaya, in 1952 the communists decided to retreat from the Bentong area in Pahang to the Betong salient in Thailand. Although sporadic acts of terror were to continue, the end of the revolt was in sight.

In 1955 a Conference of Rulers, with Johore dissenting, agreed a timetable for independence. On 31 July that year elections had been held for the Legislative Assembly. Although only one Chinese person in eight entitled to vote did so, and one Indian in seven , the result was a triumph for Tunku Abdul Rahman and for UMNO, which received 96 per cent of the votes and every seat bar one, which went to the Pan-Malayan

Islamic Party. On 28 and 29 December, the Tunku as leader of the nation met Chin Peng, who insisted on being accompanied by John Davis to ensure his security. The Tunku refused to accept the MCP as a legal political party or to vary the terms of an amnesty which he had offered. Failing agreement, Chin Peng said that the communists would cease operations after Malaya gained independence, an undertaking which he did not keep on the grounds that Commonwealth troops remained based in the country.

Much credit for defeating the communist rebellion has been given to General Gerald Templar who in 1952 was appointed both High Commissioner and Commander-in-Chief in succession to Gent and Briggs. Templar built successfully on the foundations Briggs had laid and enjoyed the military support of many Commonwealth partners, although the police proved an even more potent weapon than the soldiers. A charismatic leader, Templar played Montgomery to Briggs's Slim. Meanwhile the Tunku, as Chief Minister of the Federation, guided his people resolutely in the political battle against communism and then led the country to independence. Following a conference in London in January and February 1956, he signed on his birthday, 8 October, the formal agreement bringing British power to an end. An Independent Constitutional Commission consisting of representatives of Commonwealth countries settled the contentious issue of citizenship in February 1957 by recommending an end to dual nationality for Malaysians and making full citizenship available to people of all races who were domiciled there. On 21 August 1957 Malaya became an independent republic and elected to remain a member of the British Commonwealth. The last British troops did not leave the peninsula until 1971.

In 1949 Maurice Cotterill returned as Manager to the Kuala Reman rubber estate in Pahang from which he had fled into the jungle in 1941. The previous manager and assistant had been killed by the guerrillas. His wife Sybil and his baby daughter Philippa or Pip, did not join him until early in 1951. Although Maurice was confident that the communists would not harm him, the estate employed all the conventional means of resisting an attack, including the arming of Home Guards. For years the weekly wage money was dropped from an aircraft and Maurice travelled about in an armoured vehicle. One of Philippa's early memories is of having to puncture tins of food before they left the shop.

Maurice was exasperated by the continual strikes in the estate and, like others with experience of life before the war, did not find it easy to adapt to current labour relations, despite his deep respect for the Malayan people. He was equally out of sympathy with many European expatriates who still thought they were entitled to a privileged life. The boom in commodity prices after the outbreak of the Korean war in 1951 faded later in the decade. Estate managers came under pressure to reduce costs at a time when employees were seeking higher wages. Rubber no longer remained a monopoly product. There were other forms of elastic, such as the market leader Spandex, which had been developed in the war, and countries other than Malaya were producing latex.

Life was also difficult for Sybil Cotterill, as the only British woman on an isolated estate. She became even more lonely when

Philippa went to boarding school in Penang. Michael Thorp, who arrived as an assistant manager in February 1957, recalls Sybil as a gentle person who always wanted to talk about Britain when the assistants were invited to Maurice's bungalow for a ritual beer, but not lunch, on a Saturday. He found Maurice a less congenial companion and an unhelpful boss. Maurice had seen no reason to perpetuate the tradition that a British-owned estate should use only British managers and had wanted to appoint a local man. He resented the imposition on him of another Englishman who knew nothing about rubber planting and couldn't speak Malay. His concepts of discipline and duty were, in Thorp's view, no longer appropriate, and Thorp was not surprised when, in 1959, Maurice decided to retire a year earlier than expected. Maurice and Sybil were also unwilling to remain in Malaya when Philippa went to school in Britain.

Even at the height of the Emergency, Maurice was unwilling to say or do anything to harm the communists who had saved his life in the war, refusing to identify individual guerrillas. Thorp reports that Maurice would never speak about his wartime exploits. He showed the same reticence in Britain until the day he died in Cheshire on 8 November 1980 at the age of 74. He had by then become a pillar of the local community— a churchwarden, clerk to the Parish Council, and general doer of good works. He turned down a substantial offer to write his memoirs and refused to go on television when Spencer Chapman was featured in the programme, *This is Your Life*.

Maurice met Nona Baker again on one occasion in London when she gave him a dedicated copy of her memoirs, which were published in 1959. Like him, she had refused to say anything about her MPAJA colleagues until she knew that Lao Lee had been killed. She had by then taken a clerical job in London.

Of our other leading characters, Chin Peng is still alive, although forbidden to return to Malaya. After marrying the Air Force dispatcher who had sent him back to Malaya from Ceylon in 1945, Spencer Chapman became Organising Secretary of the Outward Bound Trust. In 1952 he, his wife, and three small children travelled by caravan across Africa. The reception of the book he wrote about the trip disappointed him. For a decade after 1956 he worked as a headmaster and in a social project in South Africa, failing to make a success of either job. In 1966 an old comrade from his wartime days found him employment as a warden of a Hall at Reading University. Feeling that the fame to which he was entitled had eluded him, he killed himself in his office there on 8 August 1971.

John Davis stayed on in the police force in Malaya after the war. After attending the Tunku's meeting with Chin Peng in 1955, he became Deputy Chairman of the War Executive Committee in Kedah. His services to Malaysia were twice honoured by the Malaysian government, adding to the Distinguished Service Order awarded by the British. He retired to Britain in 1961 and became secretary of the Kent Council of Social Services until 1974. He died in November, 2006.

Maurice Cotterill was unique as an Englishman to have lived in Malaysia while the country was successively a part of the British Empire, occupied by the Japanese, designated a British colony and then became an independent nation. He saw that men and women of all races are capable of good and evil, of generosity and greed, of kindness and cruelty, of humility and arrogance, of loyalty and treachery, of courage and cowardice. Fortunately history brings all these strands together and writes a perfect ending which, in this case, is the proud and successful Malaysian nation, celebrating its 50th year in 2007.

15

Epilogue

It was an idyllic English summer evening. The children were playing on the lawn while we and our friends sat nursing cooling drinks before enjoying supper in the garden as the sun sank behind the trees. David Gillespie had read one of my books and asked me if I had written anything else lately. I told him about *Eleven Months in Malaya*, which had been published the previous year, 2005, in Kuala Lumpur.

'My uncle was in Malaya during the war,' he said.

'When, before or after the war?'

'No, during the war. He went into the jungle when the Japanese invaded and emerged when the British returned.'

'Only three British men did that,' I replied, somewhat incredulously.

'Yes, and he was one of them.'

David then explained that his uncle, Maurice Cotterill, owed his life to those with whom he spent the war years in the jungles of Malaya. He had become opposed to colonialism and disliked the attitude of those British expatriates who thought and behaved differently. He had considered that much of what had been written about the wartime period was misleading and unfair to those involved, of whichever race. He refused to speak publicly about the Japanese occupation or the Emergency which followed, nor would he allow his memoirs to be published.

At the end of the evening, David offered to send me a copy of his uncle's wartime diary in exchange for *Eleven Months in*

Malaya, and to put me in touch with his cousin, Maurice Cotterill's only child Philippa, who had lived with her parents in Pahang after the war.

That was on 17 June 2006, 49 years after Merdeka.

Philippa read my book and kindly agreed to my using the diary to write about her father's life. My old friend, Dato' Zarir Cama, or Z as he is widely known, had been instrumental in getting *Eleven Months in Malaya* published and I told him that I thought Cotterill's diary gave a fascinating, and possibly important, insight into those turbulent times. Z suggested that, with the 50th anniversary of Malaysian independence approaching in 2007, it would be a fitting tribute to write about Maurice Cotterill's adventures and career in the context and celebration of that event.

I am grateful to Philippa, David and Z for the help they have given me. I have been unable to discover why Cotterill developed a great antipathy towards Spencer Chapman in later life. The diary gives no hint that they had fallen out and it may be that something written in *The Jungle is Neutral*, the sensational memoir published by Chapman in 1949, upset him. From Maurice's diary and Nona Baker's book, we know that *The Jungle is Neutral* contained factual errors. Chapman's dangerous habit of keeping, and losing, diaries during the war suggests that he was vain. It cannot be that Maurice was jealous of Chapman's Distinguished Service Order and bar, because he and Nona were also decorated after the war. Chapman's unhappy subsequent career and eventual suicide indicate that he had become somewhat unbalanced, but Maurice's hostility and his refusal to explain the reason for it to Philippa and

David remain a mystery.

My account of the landing at Morib, the banana money in Bidor, and the operations of the British Military Administration (BMA) rely on my own experience and that of my fellow officers, including Greig Barr, Glyn Gabe, Desmond Mangham, Philip Shimwell, and Frank Ellen. I was in charge of the guns, tanks, and other vehicles carried by sea from Madras to Morib and observed the entire landing over three days, from just offshore and by visiting the beach. I was also sent to command the small unit which processed the hundreds of Japanese surrendered personnel in Bidor. Having no civilian skills, until April 1946 I was given responsibility for preventing looting and disorder in different districts in and around Ipoh, including the Cameron Highlands and Taiping.

The routine denigration of the BMA by modern historians is misconceived. We noted how Mrs Rattray, just released from internment, criticised the Commanding Officer of the Royal Devon Yeomanry, Greig Barr, for not getting a regular bus service running from Tapah to the Cameron Highlands within two weeks of our landing, and her reference to a 'coolie woman'. In fact, the BMA repaired the infrastructure very quickly. Anyone who saw Singapore, Kuala Lumpur, Ipoh, and smaller towns in September 1945, and then saw them again six months later, as I did, would have marvelled at what had been achieved by the army and the people working together. Having served in Indian and West African Divisions, we did not think of non-Europeans as 'coolies'.

When a new management takes over an enterprise, it often seeks to present the achievements of its predecessors in disparaging terms. It appeared in April 1946 to me, and to others even better placed, that those who assumed our civil duties, many of whom had been interned in Singapore, resented not our failure but our success. They were two or three decades older than we were. They had received professional training and passed examinations, while we had not. They criticised us for not keeping records or filling in forms, while we were too short-handed to write many reports and had no forms to fill in. They damned us for letting junior officers take decisions while we saw them as bureaucrats. Many of them seemed not to have come to terms with the changed status of the European.

We, who served in the BMA, are not worried by the allegations made by the officials who replaced us, and accepted by historians, that we were incompetent and avaricious. We do, however, resent and reject an accusation of brutality. In two books recently published by academics, it is stated as fact that four demonstrators were killed when troops fired on them in Ipoh on 22 October 1945. The source of this accusation is Min Sheng Pau, a vernacular Chinese paper published in Kuala Lumpur, dated 24 October 1945. There was then no censorship and a subversive paper had no restriction on publishing rumours or lies.

None of our troops in Ipoh ever opened fire on civilians under the BMA. Apart from my own knowledge, I have spoken to Greig Barr. He states categorically that no such killing happened. If he had been personally in Tapah on that day rather than with the Regiment in Ipoh, he would have known about it. I have also spoken to Desmond Mangham, who was on that date Assistant Adjutant of the Regiment. He confirms that the allegation is false. Desmond adds that, if his or any other unit in the Division had opened fire on demonstrators, there would have been a great deal of publicity in Ipoh followed by Court of Enquiry, and there was neither. Greig later became a distinguished historian, Rector of Exeter College Oxford, and Pro-Chancellor of Oxford University. Desmond retired as a Major-General. Both are available for responsible historians to consult.

My thanks are to my neighbour, Bee Chan Steele, who translated and explained to me many Chinese and Malay expressions in the books and other papers I so much enjoyed researching; to Tim Auger whose many suggestions invariably proved helpful; and to Amirah Fatin for her interest and enthusiasm.

R.W. HOLDER
West Monkton

Glossary

BBC	British Broadcasting Corporation.
BMA	British Military Administration, the body which governed Malaya from September 1945 to April 1946.
Force 136	The special troops of the 14th Army operating behind enemy lines.
ILL	Indian Independence League.
INA	The Indian National Army, a unit raised by the Japanese from prisoners of war and local volunteers.
JIFF	A member of the Indian National Army, or Japanese/Indian Freedom Fighter.
kampong	Malay village
KMM	Kesatuan Melayu Muda, first national political organisation in British Malaya.
MCS	Malayan Civil Service.
MCP	Malayan Communist Party.
mem	term used in Malaya for a European married woman
min yuen	arm of the Malayan Communist Party
MPAJA	Malayan People's Anti-Japanese Army, mainly Chinese communist body aided by Force 136.
parang	traditional Malay dagger
RAF	Royal Air Force.
SAS	Special Air Service Regiment, elite force of the British Army.
SOE	Special Operations Executive, a British covert operations service formed in July 1940 to co-ordinate action against enemies by means of subversion, sabotage and propaganda
tuan besar	chief
UMNO	United Malays National Organisation.